LEGENDARY FOLK OF WADSWORTH OHIO

LEGENDARY FOLK OF WADSWORTH OHIO

CAESAR A. CARRINO

THE History PRESS

Published by The History Press
Charleston, SC 29403
www.historypress.net

All images are from the OZ-2 collection unless otherwise noted.

First published 2010

Manufactured in the United States

ISBN 978.1.60949.009.6

Library of Congress Cataloging-in-Publication Data

Carrino, Caesar A., 1931-
Legendary folk of Wadsworth, Ohio / Caesar A. Carrino.
p. cm.
Includes bibliographical references.
ISBN 978-1-60949-009-6
1. Wadsworth (Ohio)--Biography. 2. Wadsworth (Ohio)--History. I. Title.
F499.W13C36 2010
977.1'35--dc22
2010018258

CONTENTS

Foreword, by Lynda C. Carrino 7
Acknowledgements 9

Part I. Those Who Left Wadsworth Better than They Found It
General Elijah Wadsworth: Without Him, What Follows Wouldn't 11
Elijah Wadsworth's Contribution to the Revolutionary War 13
Move to Ohio 14
The Brouse Legacy: More than a Hill 16
Joe Bender: A Legend in His Own Time 18
The Doctors Johnson: They Gave Wadsworth More than Medicine 22
Vernon V. Isham: His Great Depression Was not *the* Great Depression 29
Captain Theodore Wolbach (1844–1928): His Life Was Not Always Picture-Perfect 33

Part II. The South End
Without It, Wadsworth Might Have Gone "South" 39
George Wise: Who Was He? 41
Dr. Hanson Hard: An Early Couch Potato 43
The Hunsbergers, Kulp and Nash: Added Utility to Comfort 45

Contents

Others Who Contributed to the South End Industrial Incubator 47
Fire Chief Harrison G. Sears: Fighting Hell with a Squirt Gun 48
The Match Shop Women: Liberated by the Match Before Women's Lib 52
William E. Artman: He Opened Many "Valves" in Wadsworth 53
The Good Folks at the Wadsworth Salvation Army 59
Hiram Yockey and the Men Who Built the Brickyard: Follow the Red Brick Road Around the World 64

Part III. Arts and Recreation
Musical Luminaries of Wadsworth 71
Emma Struggles Wuchter 72
Divas of the Opera: Not Really 73
Sports Stars and Racehorses 76
Art Wright: The "Wright" Man for the Job 80
Horse Racing: From Coal Yards to Racetracks 83
Recreation for Women 84
Prizefighting 86

Part IV. Wadsworth at Home in the Air
Early Wadsworth Housing Developments: Built and Housed Wadsworth's Legends 89
Curry, Baldwin and Brenneman: Their Air Designs Finally Took Off! 96
The Wadsworth Airport: Not "Grounded" by Stormy Opposition 99
From Model Planes to "Plane" Living 100
Post Office: Once a "Male" Thing 101
Worth Westenbarger 104

Part V. Wadsworth's Colorful Characters
Big Andy: A Sizeable Legend 109
Roy Moore: Skated into the Hearts of Wadsworth 112
Philemon Kirkum: The Beauty in the Be[a]st 115
The Kremer Legacy: Marguerite Straiton, Culture in Eight Languages 118

Bibliography 125
About the Author 127

FOREWORD

Legendary Folk of Wadsworth, Ohio, recalls stories of the people who made Wadsworth the cherished community it is today. Some of the people were legendary because they made contributions to industry or commerce; others, simply because they added to the characterization of what we know as small-town charm.

In *Remembering Wadsworth: From Pioneers to Streetcars*, Caesar Carrino chronicled the origins of Wadsworth, starting with the pioneers who first set foot in the wilderness that became Wadsworth. In this book, he spotlights some of the people who were fortunate enough to have had those pioneers make a place for them to build factories, businesses, homes and memories.

Most of the offerings herein are derived from the annals of history published in books written from 75 to 140 years ago, as well as archived newspaper articles, later publications, interviews and unpublished documents. Others, of more recent vintage, are memories the author, an eighty-year-old Wadsworth native, recalls from his earlier days. Materials that need to be factual are, indeed, from documented sources; memories are not. Yet many of the memories presented herein are etched in the minds of Wadsworthites who are in their final years of life and, therefore, could well be documented if they were written. Perhaps with this book, they will now be documented.

Foreword

Fate and Nature determine many of the world's directions. So it was with Wadsworth. Fate determined that the railroad would come through the South End of Wadsworth because trains in those days could not scale the elevation at Doylestown or traverse the terrain anywhere else in Wadsworth. Fate placed the highest grade on the railroad at Silvercreek, in a spot Nature endowed with trees that were so abundant, they could supply all the wood the trains needed. Nature also placed the coal that replaced wood as fuel at the same location.

Nature collaborated with Fate: the railroad came there, trees grew there and coal was found there. Fate and Nature provided the stage, Wadsworth's legendary people provided the drama and memories recorded it all.

Lynda C. Carrino

ACKNOWLEDGEMENTS

The author wishes to acknowledge his wife, Lynda, for her support in editing and assisting in the research for this book and for her active participation in the Wadsworth Area Historical Society. Her prowess as a historian guided him in finding little-known facts in obscure locations.

Appreciation is offered also to Michael Carrino for his computer technology assistance, particularly in devising strategies to save time, energy and patience.

Thanks are given to the scores of Wadsworth residents who encouraged the author to write a complement to his previous book, *Remembering Wadsworth: From Pioneers to Streetcars.*

Finally, credit is given to OZ-2 Productions of Wadsworth for supplying most of the pictures used for the various chronicles and for its technical assistance, to the Wadsworth Area Historical Society for additional pictures and to others whose pictures will be identified when used.

PART I

THOSE WHO LEFT WADSWORTH BETTER THAN THEY FOUND IT

General Elijah Wadsworth

Without Him, What Follows Wouldn't

No history of Wadsworth would be complete without referring to the person after whom it was named: General Elijah Wadsworth.

Elijah came from a long line of wealthy people in Connecticut, originating from one of the founders of Hartford, Connecticut: William Wadsworth. William had many descendants, many of whom were noted for their historic value in the early days of the formation of our country.

Elijah was related to Henry Wadsworth Longfellow, the literary giant—or perhaps one should say that Henry was related to Elijah, since Elijah preceded Henry. Elijah was born on November 4, 1747, to Joseph III and Elizabeth Cook Wadsworth. Henry Wadsworth Longfellow was born on February 27, 1807, sixty years later. The "Wadsworth" in Henry's name came from his mother's side of the family; she was the former Zilpah Wadsworth, married to Henry's father, Stephen Longfellow. Zilpah's ancestors originated from the same Wadsworth family.

In Connecticut, the Wadsworths made the history that Wadsworth High School students read today without being aware that Elijah was a direct descendant of this history-making family.

The Charter Oak was the tree in which General Elijah Wadsworth's great-grandfather hid the Connecticut Charter to conceal it from the British, who wanted to destroy it.

Elijah's great-grandfather Joseph is the one who is associated with the Charter Oak. A quick review of the history of the tree would remind the reader that the Constitution Charter was hidden inside a cavity in the tree to keep it safe from the then appointee of King James II of England, Sir Edmund Andros, who was sent to govern the five states that we call New England.

Going back a little in history, in 1662, King Charles II of England granted the Connecticut Colony more autonomy than it had previously enjoyed and sealed his agreement with Connecticut in a document known as the Constitution Charter (Connecticut Charter). After King Charles II died, his successor, King James II, wanted to rescind the charter and ordered it seized. The people of Connecticut were violently opposed to this and made every effort to keep the charter from the king. A verbal battle ensued, but the king had more power than the citizens and told them if they did not surrender it voluntarily, he would dissolve Connecticut and parcel it out to Massachusetts and New York.

In the meantime, King James II appointed Sir Edmund Andros to govern the newly formed New England states. On October 26, 1687, Andros went to Butler's Tavern in Hartford (now Connecticut's capital) to retrieve the charter. The people fought giving it up, knowing their freedom would be curtailed were it revoked. In fact, had that happened, Connecticut would probably not be a state today. The council argued with Andros, and "mysteriously" the candles and lanterns went out during the discussion. This is "mysterious" because there was no master switch to extinguish them; several people had to act in unison to put the chambers into darkness.

Captain Joseph Wadsworth was waiting outside, saddled on his horse. In an instant, the charter was slipped to him, whereupon he rode "with fury and conviction" to the Wylls estate in Hartford, where he knew there was a huge oak tree. He looked for an opening in the tree and hid the document inside. From that point on, history has called this tree the Charter Oak.

Because the council members knew that Andros had power over them, they did not want to disquiet him by not having the charter there when the lights were reignited. To accomplish this, the council had made an impeccably high-quality fake copy, therein giving the illusion that it was still there when the candles and lamps were relit. Whether Andros ever learned that he had been duped is not recorded.

As a point of interest, the Charter Oak tree did not succumb to old age until 150 years after Joseph Wadsworth put the true charter papers inside it. When it blew down, wood from the oak was made into a chair that now resides in the Capitol Building in Hartford, Connecticut. It is estimated the oak could have been almost 450 years old when it fell.

Elijah Wadsworth's Contribution to the Revolutionary War

Elijah Wadsworth volunteered in the Revolutionary War after he heard about the Battle of Bunker Hill. He served as a lieutenant under Captain Benjamin Tallmadge (Tallmadge, Ohio, was named after him but was founded by the Reverend David Bacon). Although this battle was fought in Boston and not in Connecticut, Elijah was deeply disturbed that the British had twenty-four hundred troops and the American Continental army only twelve hundred. Still, while the British army may have been regaled in military splendor with cannons and guns, the Continental army, armed with muskets and uniformed in whatever clothes it could find, fought valiantly. Elijah was impressed and wanted to be a part of the action.

Elijah distinguished himself quickly and was put in charge of the guards who held Major John Andre after he was arrested and before his trial. The reader will remember that Major Andre was highly admired by General George Washington for being an outstanding soldier, but the general was shocked and disconsolate when he learned that Andre had become a cunning spy who contrived with Benedict Arnold, another historical traitor, to undermine the Continental army by offering help to the British for money.

Since Andre was of such high profile, it was necessary for the captain of the guard to be of impeccable character. It is for this reason that Elijah Wadsworth was chosen for the position. The trial was the focal point of the news of the day and ended with Andre being hanged as a traitor. Once again, a Wadsworth name became associated with the early history of our land.

MOVE TO OHIO

As was mentioned earlier, Elijah Wadsworth came from wealth. He was part owner of the Connecticut Land Company and had ready access to prime locations. The northern boundary of the company was Lake Erie, and the southern, the Medina-Wayne County Line Road, known to Wadsworth residents as Eastern Road. The western boundary extended 120 miles from the western Pennsylvania border.

When the Connecticut Land Company began selling huge plats of land from its vast holdings, Elijah bought one of the largest: the plat in which Wadsworth was located. He actually owned land from west of Wadsworth to the Pennsylvania border.

In 1799, when Elijah was fifty-four, he moved to the newly purchased investment in Ohio and made his home in Warren for a short time. He then moved to Canfield, which became his permanent residence, and constructed the first wood-frame home built in Ohio in October 1802. The house still stands today.

It did not take long for Wadsworth to make his presence felt in Canfield. He organized the government there, established the first post office, built the school and formed a militia. Despite the fact he did not settle in Wadsworth, he maintained a strong interest in the town because he owned nearly all of the surrounding land. He was impressed with the fact that the first settlers *chose* to settle in what we now know as Wadsworth—settlers who came from his home state near where he was born. He encouraged more people to join the few pioneers who sawed and chopped their way from Connecticut to Wadsworth. So great was his concern for Wadsworth that the newly arrived families named the town after him. Wadsworth, however, never lived in the city that bears his name

By the time the War of 1812 broke out, Elijah Wadsworth had achieved the rank of general, a title that followed him for the rest of his life. Having moved here in 1799, he was now an Ohioan. Shortly after the war began, Elijah built the militia in northeast Ohio by recruiting and organizing three thousand men and assuming the responsibility for the defense of one-third of the state of Ohio. He ordered several forts and bunkers to be constructed for the protection of the citizens and built roads so he could go from place to place between commands. He personally took command at the Battle of the Peninsula on September 10, 1812, a battle that was waged at the mouth of the Huron River. Because of age and failing health, he had to resign his position in February 1814, before the end of the war.

Another interesting bit of trivia about General Wadsworth is that his home in Litchfield, Connecticut, was purchased by Presbyterian minister Dr. Lyman Beecher, the father of Henry Ward Beecher and Harriet Beecher Stowe, two great giants in American literature. Also in this house, another part of American history was born: the American Temperance Society, an organization that flourished for many years to curb, if not outlaw, intoxicating beverages. This might well have been the genesis of the swelling temperance movement that culminated, in 1920, in the enactment of the Eighteenth Amendment to the Constitution—the Prohibition Act—which was repealed by the Twenty-third Amendment in 1933.

There is a monument honoring General Elijah Wadsworth on the greens in Canfield, located in the center of town and on the north side of Route 224. The Wadsworth Museum is on the south side of Route 224, almost across from the monument. A short distance south of the museum is the house Wadsworth built; it has had some remodeling and updating but is essentially in the same condition as when it was built in 1802.

The house was big by 1802 standards—and perhaps even by some of today's standards. The first floor has the usual types of rooms: a kitchen (fairly large), a dining room, a sitting room, a parlor and some smaller closet-type rooms. The second story has bedrooms that are minimally commodious and not elegant, ceilings that are not nearly as high as the ones on the first floor and evidence of nooks where small heating stoves might have been placed.

General Elijah Wadsworth died at his home in Canfield, Ohio, on December 30, 1817, at age seventy.

THE BROUSE LEGACY

More than a Hill

Brouse Hill, Brouse Drive, Brouse Farm. All of these emanated from one person: William Franklin Brouse, who was born on July 9, 1841, the son of William and Rebecca, in Chippewa Township, across the South Medina-Wayne County Road.

Will Brouse, as he was known to old-timers, came to the northern extremes of Wadsworth when he was one year old. The present farm is still an expansive acreage with trees, but only where the owners want them; when Will came, trees were everywhere nature wanted them. In order to till the land, the Brouses had to fell the trees one by one. Each tree took about a day's work since they were so large. Additionally, they were almost all hardwood.

Will remembered when his father planted small fields of grain where the trees had been cleared. He had to shoo away the hundreds of pigeons that would pick up the kernels of grain as fast as they were broadcast onto the ground.

It took years to clear the land to its present almost-treeless condition, done by human perspiration and mighty oxen. Will was relegated the task of breaking up the virgin soil with oxen, after which his father would "plow" the field for crops. The oxen were strong enough to cut through the roots that remained from the trees that had been cleared away.

On October 4, 1862, Will brought Barbara M. Bair into the family as his wife. Three children were the products of this marriage: Elmer, Grace and Elnoria. Elmer, Grace and Barbara preceded Will in death.

The Brouse House stood as a beacon on top of a hill aptly known as Brouse Hill. The house is no longer there.

In 1886, Will built a house on the hill, a beacon of the past that stood near the water tower. It was last inhabited by a Brouse descendant, Lloyd Brouse, a bachelor who lived there until he died. Lloyd was a quiet man, drove a Model A Ford coupe and didn't "go" much, except to town to get supplies. He commanded respect through his nonthreatening personality and hard work, therein maintaining the legacy of the long-standing Brouse tradition in Wadsworth. Many other Brouse descendants remain, great-great- and great-great-great-grand-relatives of Will's.

In Will's obituary in 1929, there was a notation about his having followed the "simple life of a pioneer so far as habits were concerned, but in industry, he was modern and progressive." Will translated these qualities into values for his progeny. Wadsworth residents would make this claim about any of the Brouse descendants. Will was survived by only one brother, M.D. Brouse. Seven other siblings preceded him in death.

Following World War II, houses were built north and south of Route 261 on a portion of the Brouse Farm and on the Dohner Farm. The Dohners entered the Brouse family when Elnoria married Charles Dohner, her second husband. She first married David Long, but according to accounts, David did not stay with his family. Lloyd Brouse and his sister, Lula, were offspring of David and Elnoria's marriage.

Charles died in 1936, and Elnoria followed in 1952 at age eighty-six. They had three girls: Grace (d. 1996), Ruth (d. 1995) and Idell (d. 2004). Much of the original farm still remains in the family despite the death of many of the earlier descendants. Dohner Drive was named for the family, as was Brouse Drive.

According to a family member, Johnny Hayne (married to a Brouse descendant, Faith Richel; both are now deceased), the first "leg" of the barn on the farm was built in 1832. In subsequent years, extensions were added to the existing structure. This would imply that someone else had owned the farm previously, since the Brouses did not move there until 1842. Documentation is sketchy about ownership, but Edward Brown's *Wadsworth Memorial*, published in 1875, places Abel Beach (father of Sylvia Beach, who was lost and never found) on what was later the Brouse Farm in 1823. There are no records of anyone else having owned it before the Beaches did. It can be assumed they purchased the land from the Connecticut Land Company. It is also possible they are the ones who built the first "leg" of the barn in 1832.

There is evidence the Frank family lived on the farm at one time; however, the dates of habitation overlap somewhat. One explanation could be that the Franks lived there when the Brouse family moved to Illinois for a period of time.

JOE BENDER

A Legend in His Own Time

Few people in Wadsworth came from Switzerland, but Joe Bender's parents did. Moriz Bender brought his wife, Agatha Meyer Bender, to Wadsworth from that mountainous country in 1867 to ply his trade as a cobbler. Cobblers in those days did more than repair shoes; they made them as well. It was a good trade, but it paid poorly, particularly since there were so many cobblers to service so few people.

Joe Bender's parents lived in one of a group of small houses to the rear and east of what is now St. Mark's Church but was then the First Mennonite Church. The area has since been known as Bender's Court, giving evidence to where the family lived for many years. Joe was born there in 1880. None of the original houses remains.

Joe didn't want to become a cobbler but worked in the shop with his father as a helper. Stories he told revealed that he could repair shoes if he had to, but he didn't want to. Instead, to earn the few pennies a day he made, he chose to shoo flies from horses for the blacksmith who lived near his house. But he didn't want to do that for the rest of his life, either.

Joe could be considered one of the charter members of workers who spent long hours at monotonous jobs at the "Match," known officially as the Ohio Match Company. He began working at the Match in 1898, when the company had been in operation for only a few short years, and earned only five cents an hour for his work. After several years of this monotony, he didn't want to be confined there for life, so he made inroads to become a foreman over some of the machine operators. He worked long hours and learned all there was to know about the machinery. Finally, he was promoted and began earning twenty cents an hour, a huge jump from the five cents per hour he had earned as a laborer.

From an early age, Joe knew what he wanted and worked hard to get it. He took the twenty cents an hour, saved as much as he could and bought a popcorn wagon, which he would push onto the square in the evenings and on Saturdays. This added to his income. Also, in April 1907, he became the ticket taker on the first streetcar that came into Wadsworth and served in that capacity for a time. It is doubtful he earned much with this new job since the fare was between five and ten cents from Wadsworth to Barberton. When he thought he had enough money to do so, he married Kathryn McDermott from Doylestown and settled in Wadsworth for good.

Joe and Katy never had children but nurtured and provided for hundreds of children throughout their many years of marriage. They opened Bender's Restaurant, located on the north side of College Street, west of the Myers Block building (on the corner of High and College Streets), and served wholesome meals to patrons—never fancy, just wholesome. More important than the fact that they owned a restaurant is that they made sure people who did not have food received it through their private, quiet and selfless sharing with the poor.

Many stories abound about the restaurant. Meals were very inexpensive because Katy would cook and Joe would serve. Occasionally, there would be other waitresses, but Joe kept the overhead down with his and Katy's personal involvement. Atmosphere was not their goal; serving good, wholesome and inexpensive food was. The story goes that one time a person asked for a piece of raisin pie. Joe said the pie wasn't raisin and shooed the flies away. There is no documentation to this story, and it is highly possible that it was one of the many made-up stories that prevailed around Wadsworth when entertainment was lacking and creativity was high. Nonetheless, the story has survived to this day.

During the Depression, Joe purchased many houses in Wadsworth that were being foreclosed. According to relatives, Joe would permit the people to then live in the houses they had just lost and charged little or no rent. The reason this documentation had to come from relatives is that Joe and Katy never flaunted their charitable deeds. In fact, they would all but deny their largesse.

Joe and Katy were both very religious, attending Mass at Sacred Heart Church on a daily basis, working for the church, singing in the choir, presenting programs for church functions, cooking church dinners, serving at funeral luncheons and doing everything from cleaning the church to giving considerable pieces of land for Sacred Heart School and donating their house to the church upon death. Christmas parties were not complete without Joe's reciting poetry from memory or presenting a reading from one of Shakespeare's works, skills he learned during the days he was an actor on the legitimate Wadsworth stage.

In 1913, Joe purchased the Opera House, a theatre that hosted live shows and noted speakers for several years before it was torn down. The theatre was built in 1895 by Dr. Detweiler, who sold it before he had to make major repairs and accommodations to serve a newer brand of performances. Although this was not the first gesture of service Joe shared with the community, it was a significant one that evinced acclaim from a wide audience ready for a higher level of entertainment. Joe was one of the entertainers. With a stentorian vocal prowess and an uncanny ability to memorize vast quantities of script, he performed almost endlessly as a Shakespearean actor. He carried those lines to his death, performing at the slightest request. He also played other roles that were not so classical.

Joe gave land to the city on two occasions: he donated a piece of property that went from Humbolt Street to Crestwood Avenue through Durling Park and a piece of land at the end of East Street for the city to build a bridge over the railroad tracks so firefighting equipment could traverse the railroad tracks if a train were blocking the Main Street crossing. The city used the land for the road through the park but not that at the end of East Street for the bridge.

Joe Bender started at the very bottom and finished at the top, always sharing his fortune with untold numbers.

Joe was not a model of sartorial elegance. He dressed up to go to church or to social functions but was most comfortable in work clothes or painter's overalls. On one occasion, an eyewitness recounts that Joe went to the First National Bank in Norton on a busy Friday afternoon. As he entered, the manager spotted him in his well-worn and soiled work clothes. According to the story, the bank manager was talking with a customer and uttered in a soft voice, "Here comes another one to hit us up for a ten or a five." The customer happened to be from Wadsworth and knew Joe. Without hesitation, the customer told the manager who Joe was and that he should be careful about what he was saying because Joe was far from poor. With that, the manager walked over to Joe and greeted him as if he were a welcomed customer rather than a panhandler. Joe asked the manager what his function in the bank was, and upon learning that he was indeed the manager, Joe said that that was whom he had come to see. Several weeks later, the customer to whom the manager had been talking when Joe walked in came back to the bank. The manager walked over to him and thanked him profusely for alerting him to Joe's financial status. Although details were not revealed, there was no question about what was implied in the manager's comments of appreciation.

Joe and his brother, Charlie, were both firemen. It was not unusual to see Joe on the fire truck, even in his advanced years. Some said he did it for the miserly pittance volunteer firemen got when they went to a fire—a dollar or two. The truth is, Joe knew he had only a little time left to serve the community he loved, and he was going to serve it until he could no longer do so.

When Joe died, residents asked, "How much did he leave?" The answer was simple: all of it. He took nothing with him except the respect, appreciation and adulation of a community that was richer for his having lived there for eighty-seven years.

THE DOCTORS JOHNSON

They Gave Wadsworth More than Medicine

Father and son teams of doctors are quite common; father and daughter combinations are not. Wadsworth had one such uncommon team: Dr. Robert L. Johnson and his daughter, Dr. Myra Johnson.

Both Dr. Johnsons carved niches into Wadsworth lore in their own right. Dr. Robert was not only a respected physician but a community leader as well. He was mayor of Wadsworth from 1906 through the end of his second term, four years later. He pounded the "golden" spike into the ties when the streetcar line was completed in 1907. The spike was not really gold. It was called so because of the famed "golden spike" that was pounded into the railroad ties that connected the West to the East. In truth, Dr. Johnson pounded the *last* spike to be driven into the ties. Conservative Wadsworthites would never have allowed a golden spike to be pounded into the tracks—or anywhere else, for that matter.

Mayor Robert Johnson preparing to pound the last spike into the ties for the streetcar tracks at the square in 1907.

Dr. Robert resided just north of the square in a house that was built by carriage maker H.J. Traver, whose carriage shop was across the street from the house. Dr. Robert was the third doctor in the house that had been vacated by Traver many years earlier. Dr. Myra was the fourth.

Dr. Robert did not just "happen" to come to Wadsworth. In fact, he had never heard of Wadsworth until Wadsworth native Dr. Wilbert Hinsdale, then dean of the University of Michigan Medical School where R.L. Johnson was a student, recommended it. Dr. Hinsdale recognized the qualities in Dr. R.L. Johnson to be in step with what Wadsworth needed and pointed him here in 1900. Dr. Johnson, a brilliant student (as reported by those who knew him), was only twenty-two years old when he came to Wadsworth in 1900. He was born in Vassar, Michigan, in 1878 and graduated from the University of Michigan Medical School in 1899.

Wadsworth had physicians practicing here; some were even graduates of medical schools. Many others served apprenticeships with doctors. Even in those early days, physicians began to understand that they needed more than an "apprenticeship" with another physician to be competent in the growing science of medicine. Dr. Johnson's degree from the University of Michigan was most impressive, signifying that he was a learned scholar in medical science from a highly respected institution.

Wadsworth was small in the early part of the century; it would not reach the mandated five thousand inhabitants to become a city until 1931. Sick people depended on the accepted medical wisdom of the day, many times without positive results. Dr. Johnson was young, strong and qualified in then state-of-the-art medicine. People sometimes found it difficult to come to him, so he went to them in horse and buggy at first and later by car. He was indeed a country doctor, an apt description since he was a doctor who served an agrarian population.

Old-timers remember the countless stories of how some doctors cured pneumonia with corn plasters, consumption (tuberculosis) with fresh air, inflammation of the bowels (a type of cancer) with herbs and hardening of the arteries (atherosclerosis) with a pronouncement that death would come soon. Dr. Johnson brought his skill as a diagnostician and treating physician to a community that was emerging from the medical practices cited above—albeit cautiously, since some of the earlier remedies were effective. In essence, he and a couple other university-trained physicians added newer procedures for curing the sick.

Dr. Johnson had an approach that could have been interpreted as frightening; however, close friends acclaimed his gentleness, warmth, compassion and caring. He was direct, a gene he passed on to his daughter, Dr. Myra. He was dedicated, another gene he gave Dr. Myra. Dr. Robert knew every patient as a person and knew peculiarities about each one. There is one story about a woman who called him in the middle of the night during a snowstorm to report that the neighbor across the road was about to give birth. Dr. Johnson went to the caller's house because he recognized her voice. He apologized to the lady for awakening her but was happy she was not the one giving birth because he knew she couldn't any more. When he went to the neighbor's house to deliver the baby, the mother was in the last stages of birth. He delivered the baby and then gave instructions to the father about what to do next because he had to leave before the driving snow covered the tracks he had made on the way to the house.

World War I found Dr. Johnson in another role: physician in the military. He served as a captain. He stayed in the service of his country until the war ended in 1918 and then returned to Wadsworth to continue his practice. Following his return, he worked closely with other doctors and community leaders to transform the Ohio Match horse barn into a hospital. Before that, "hospitals" were in the homes of some of the doctors. Dr. Bolich's was one such home. According to a granddaughter, Dr. Bolich was motivated to find another venue for a hospital when his wife feared coming down the stairs some morning to find one of the patients dead on a cot in her dining room.

Dr. Johnson was a very persuasive and tenacious person. His efforts, in concert with those cited above, finally convinced the Young family to part with the horse barn so that the city could use it for a hospital. Since horses were quickly falling into disuse and the barn was no longer needed, the Match owners acceded. Dr. Johnson served as the chair of the hospital staff for years and even served as its spiritual leader, another testament to his compassionate nature.

Dr. Hinsdale's directing Dr. Johnson to Wadsworth not only gave Wadsworth another doctor but also put Dr. Johnson in a position to marry one of the local girls, Beulah Koplin. He and Beulah had two daughters, Kathleen and Myra. Kathleen did not remain in Wadsworth, but Dr. Myra returned to her homestead after serving in other locations for a period of time. She lived in the upstairs of the homestead and maintained the downstairs for her office, just as her father had. The only difference was that when Dr. Robert was there, he had a wife and two daughters living in the house. Dr. Myra lived alone, never having married. She actually lived in the house until she died, so it would be appropriate to say she was born and died in the house where she lived the majority of her life.

Dr. Myra was a direct person who could strike fear in her opponents but commanded the respect and admiration of her patients and colleagues. Other doctors would laud her but, at the same time, relate "interesting" stories about her approach to problems, both medical and social. She had a great sense of humor and loved the people she considered close friends.

There are as many stories about Dr. Myra as there are people telling them, but one has been told time and time again. During one of the mayoral campaigns several years ago, the Democratic candidate, J.D. Henson, was campaigning on a Saturday afternoon through the downtown. This did not attract too much attention, but the fact that he had a donkey with him (the mascot of the Democratic Party) did. Candidate Henson went down Main Street on the east side, crossed over to the west side and walked all the way to the Lutheran church, going into some of the stores along the way with the donkey. When he got to the Lutheran church, he crossed the street to go down High Street on the east side, whereupon, Dr. Myra came out with a camera and called: "J. D., get over here. I want to take your picture." Dr. Myra's tone left no question in J.D.'s mind that he needed to accede to her demand. As he and his co-worker walked up the sidewalk to get close enough for the picture, Dr. Myra snapped, "Put the jackass in the middle so I can take the picture." With this, J.D. put the donkey in the middle; he stood to one side, and the co-worker stood to the other. Without hesitation, Dr. Myra scolded: "I said, didn't you hear me, I said get in the middle, J.D."

Without going into further detail about the demeanor of this fourth-generation physician to occupy the Traver House, the reader should arrive at a conclusion that would give an accurate representation of Dr. Myra Johnson's personality.

Dr. Myra had a playful side to an otherwise austere and commanding presence. She had a horn on her car that produced a horse's whinny, surprising nearly everyone—especially those who knew only her harsher side. Although she would never have purchased such a horn, she had it installed in her car because it was a gift from an admiring friend.

Dr. Myra had close friends, among them Merle Wearstler, the wife of Wadsworth dentist Dr. David Wearstler. Their friendship emanated from the close friendship Dr. Myra had with the Wearstlers' daughter, Cindy Riggs. In a letter Merle wrote of memories she had about her good friend, she tells about Dr. Myra coming to her house for dinner at Halloween with her French poodle, Beau, which she carried into the house. The dog was attached to Dr. Myra and was quite timid with strangers; hence, it stayed on her lap during the beginning of the visit. After a fairly long time, the poodle became a little more accustomed to the surroundings and began wandering inquisitively around the house. Suddenly, with a bolt and a leap, the dog jumped into Dr. Myra's lap with such force that it knocked the wind out of

Dr. Myra Johnson was the daughter of Dr. Robert Johnson and practiced in the same house as her father until she died.

her. Following the dog was a "ghost" in the form of Cindy, who had a sheet covering her entire body. Although windless, Dr. Myra was able to conjure up one of her hearty laughs.

Dr. Myra's more artistic side was dedicated to music, a passion that was enhanced by a record player she purchased with a gift she received from a Smith College friend who had no family. The friend was blessed with means and gave large monetary gifts to various friends at Christmas. Dr. Myra was one of these friends but refused to accept the gifts. After much entreating, she finally accepted $100, the amount she needed to purchase the record player and some operatic records and books, her other passion. It is a known fact that Dr. Myra spent little money on anything except music, books and art.

Dr. Myra was a gourmet cook. She frequently invited friends to her home for dinner and presented a table that was replete with fresh flowers—usually roses from her garden, when in season—fine linens and china and the most delicious food a palate could taste. Friends waited for invitations and were never disappointed with the novelty or the quality of the dinner. Dr. Myra cooked all this on an antique gas stove, a relic of the 1910s that had been in the family for years and with which she never parted. Dinner was served on dining room furniture that was of the English style and in heavy dark oak.

Despite the inconvenience of not having access to the cellar from the main house, she never made the adjustment that would have precluded her from having to go outside the kitchen door to enter another door to go into the basement. The basement was as it had been originally. Today, the beams (actually, big, long, straight logs) still have the bark on them that covered them in 1850. To accommodate the "modern" furnace—previous heating came from parlor stoves—a portion of the basement had to be excavated,

Dr. Robert Johnson's funeral. The man at the rear of the casket is Dr. Paul Goss, a longtime Wadsworth dentist.

further emphasizing the rustic configuration of the original cellar. This is yet another example of how Dr. Myra lived her life: as she wanted to and without flourish.

Both Dr. Johnsons left a legacy that still lives in Wadsworth. The latest is that the Wadsworth Area Historical House is located in the Traver-Johnson House. Despite the fact that Dr. Robert died nearly sixty years ago, and Dr. Myra more than ten, the house invites stories about them that are endless.

Few people can claim this honor. Fewer still deserve it.

Vernon V. Isham

His Great Depression Was not the *Great Depression*

The only school in Wadsworth named for a person is Isham Memorial School, more commonly called Isham School. Owen J. Work had an auditorium named in his honor, and Arthur Wright, a stadium.

Vernon V. Isham, superintendent and principal of Wadsworth Centralized School (formerly, Wadsworth Township School) from 1931 until his death in 1957, was a legacy in his own time, but now his legacy lives on in a school named in his honor.

During his twenty-six-year tenure—if one includes the years he served in the military, from 1941 to 1945—he established himself as a strict, disciplined and strong leader.

Every summer in the early days of his administration, Mr. Isham drove every road in the township to take a count of who would be starting school that fall, who would not be returning as a result of having reached age sixteen (and therefore no longer required to attend school) and who had moved into the community and was not attending school. He was particularly interested in knowing how many would be going to Wadsworth High School in grades ten through twelve since the township paid tuition to the city school for those students. There is no evidence of such a census having ever been attempted before this. Collecting accurate and timely information was another mark of Vernon V. Isham's legacy.

He had a reputation for being stern and task-oriented. Those who knew him knew him only as an administrator in that he did not encourage an aura of closeness with students.

Vernon V. Isham was rewarded for his good works with the school where he was principal when it was named in his honor.

Most students had a distant respect for him; some even feared him. It was not unusual to glimpse the paddle he kept in his left hip pocket when his suit coat would flip back. He drove a 1936 light green Chevrolet coupe during the late '30s and '40s. When his car pulled into the school drive during recess, a pall of hushed anxiety would spread over the student body.

Most of the perceptions of Mr. Isham were made by the students themselves. Teachers respected him, and parents believed in him and followed him. As evidence of the latter, consider that in 1938, when the country was still in the depths of the Great Depression, he was able to pass a bond issue to build an addition to the west side of the school. In better times, two previous attempts had failed, but with facts on his side and an ever-increasing enrollment pushing out the walls of a school built in 1924, he was able to convince an impoverished community to sacrifice $20,000 it didn't have for the addition.

Part of his magic in convincing the public to vote for the $20,000 tax was that he applied for, and was granted, a $16,000 contribution from the Works Progress Administration (WPA) to make up the difference between the $20,000 and the $36,000 needed to complete the building project. Even if we assume today's dollar to be ten times that amount, that would translate into a $200,000 bond issue—a sizeable amount. Given the fact that there was no money anywhere, there were no jobs to make any money and almost every family had been at near-starvation levels for about nine years, winning a bond issue totaling $20,000 was an unparalleled achievement.

World War II found Isham in a military uniform for four years. During this hiatus, the school was administered by Mabel Hindman (later Becker) for two years, and then by Eugenia Foote for two years. Miss Hindman, with emphasis on *Miss*, married quite late in life, since during the Depression many schools—including Wadsworth Centralized School—forbade married females to teach unless they had been married before the Depression and were still teaching when the Depression started. Sadly, shortly after she was married, Miss Hindman's husband went to a Wadsworth doctor for a routine checkup, learned he was fine, walked out of the doctor's office and dropped dead in the doorway of the doctor's office.

Vernon V. Isham returned to the school following his discharge from the service and faced the growing problems of the postwar period. Shortly after his return, the State of Ohio began the great consolidation effort to combine all of the little schools into bigger districts. From over twenty-four hundred districts— huge, large, big, small and tiny—slightly more than six hundred districts were created.

Only the city schools escaped this process; nearly every other school in the state underwent consolidation. This was a change of such magnitude that it was tantamount to turning the entire state's historic school district model upside down. It took years, and Vernon V. Isham suffered and fought every inch of the many battles that ensued. What was to happen to Wadsworth's little township school? It flew under the banner of the Medina County Board of Education, the same jurisdiction that could make it part of any other county district in the area. Would it become a county school and be placed many miles away, or would Sharon Township, Wadsworth Township and Guilford Township (Seville) Schools combine and build a new school somewhere other than Wadsworth?

With the exception of Brunswick Schools (which had a meteoric growth spurt after World War II and soon would become a city), Medina City Schools and Wadsworth City Schools, all the other schools in Medina County consolidated into the Black River, Cloverleaf, Buckeye and Highland School Districts.

Vernon V. Isham stood alone against all odds and presented a practical solution to his board: merge Wadsworth Centralized School with Wadsworth City Schools. The board was reluctant to make such a move and opted to put it to the voters. Once again, the people's trust in Isham prevailed. The electorate passed the merger option, and in 1957, all schools in Wadsworth were placed under the city school system.

Had Isham not initiated this move, Wadsworth City Schools would have suffered significantly, since the state withdrew funds from the township to pay the city schools tuition for students in grades ten through twelve, a covenant initiated in 1927. Although it was not documented, people in Wadsworth believed the state withdrew the funds to force the separation of the township school from Wadsworth City Schools, a move that would have forced Wadsworth Centralized to merge with one of the other districts cited above.

Isham began to feel isolated in his plight: the board was hesitant to move forward with the township/city merger option, the county was putting pressure on him to consolidate with other township schools, the state took away his money and his superintendent colleagues felt he was disavowing them by not joining with them in the consolidation movement. But in typical Isham style, he showed no emotion—only leadership. Those working around him at the time did not notice any evidence of his being overwhelmed; rather, they thought he was more pensive that usual, probably trying to sort out all the options in a practical and logical manner. Even after the victory—a several-year ordeal—he dropped the consolidation issue immediately and tackled the next problem on his desk, all without fanfare or notoriety.

What follows might explain the "pensive" demeanor described in the paragraph above. Vernon V. Isham was a very private man, especially about his many heartaches. He was married to Miriam Fenstemaker Isham for many years, but they did not have children until late in their marriage. After he returned from the service, they were blessed with the birth of a baby girl, who unfortunately never walked, talked or was able to care for herself. After twelve years in this sad condition, she died, just as she was ready to mature. According to Miriam—with whom this writer spent many months in graduate classes—the child was not able to physically accommodate the bodily changes that presented themselves at puberty. Shortly thereafter, on July 14, 1957, Vernon V. Isham died suddenly. Again according to Miriam, he died from a heartbreak that belied this stern, disciplined and task-oriented man, one that he never let anyone know he had. He had cared for his baby daughter more than anything else in life, and now that she was no longer living, he didn't want to be either. Miriam's heart went with both of them and stayed there until she died a few years later— also of heartbreak.

The travails of administrative loneliness and unending battles that would have weakened anyone else did not take him; Vernon V. Isham succumbed to grief over a daughter who never lived, even before she died.

Captain Theodore Wolbach (1844–1928)

His Life Was Not Always Picture-Perfect

When the phonograph was first invented by Thomas Edison, people would say they had an Edison. Later, when RCA Victor introduced the Victrola, the trade name for its model of phonograph, people started calling phonographs victrolas. When Westinghouse used the word "fridgidaire" in promoting its refrigerators, some people used that term for all refrigerators. Many people still call copies of original documents Xerox copies, using the trade name of only one of many copying machines.

So it was with Wolbach. Theodore Wolbach had a camera—a primitive one, to be sure—but he had it with him everywhere he went. He was highly regarded as a photographer, and people in Wadsworth began calling pictures that came from cameras "Wolbach pictures," probably because he was the lone practitioner in this new medium.

But Wolbach's life was not always picture-perfect. In fact, it was riddled with sadness, strife, poverty and heartbreak. He was born in Smithville,

Ohio, to a Jewish father and a Scotch-German mother. His father died from cholera—called the "black cholera" then—when Ted was ten years old. As one of eight children, his mother could not care for them, so she placed them with strangers who would take them and rear them as their own. Unfortunately, Ted was given to a family in Wadsworth that was extremely cruel to him, so he ran away after suffering the pain of being mistreated for a year or more. He found his way to Wooster, near to where he was born in Smithville, and despite being only twelve years old, was able to find work in a rope factory. He earned $3.75 per month plus room and board. He knew his mother lived nearby, so he had all his wages sent to her since she was struggling mightily with almost no other source of income. His heart was always with his mother; he never could accept the pain of separation.

There were those who took pity on this waif, one being a man who felt such compassion for a boy who worked so hard to help support his mother that he gave Ted a quarter to go to the Wooster (Wayne County) Fair. Ted had not seen this kind of generosity before, and certainly not in the quantity he had in his hand. A quarter is about what he would make in two days at his job.

Ted was so struck by having this much money that he trembled at the thought of spending it. He was tempted by the grand array of events in his sight but couldn't find it within himself to part with his money. Finally, after agonizing over his dilemma, he turned away from all the glitter of the fair—walking by the food, the displays, the entertainment and the crowds of people enjoying themselves—and found his way to where his mother was living. He gave her the quarter. His words are heart-rending: *"Even as a small boy, my mother's worries over financial matters affected me deeply, and I was never able to shake off this responsibility."*

Ted's education was extremely limited. He had only one year of formal education, and that only because he took a job as the janitor of a school in Wooster, carrying in coal and wood for the heating stove, cleaning the entire school and building the fire in the school during cold weather. This was a daunting level of responsibility for a child who had almost no home life, little food, meager clothing and a separated and therefore a nonexistent family life. Yet, he was grateful for the opportunity because he at least had a chance to learn, if not formally, then through the books in the students' and teachers' desks he would attempt to read.

Despite his lack of education, Ted was articulate and was able to speak on a wide range of topics. In fact, according to friends, he excelled in this to a point that the general public thought he had a fair amount of education.

His tenure at the school lasted for a couple years, but his zeal for personal advancement was compelling. He sought after and was given a job in an ambrotype gallery, something akin to a photography studio. This was the beginning of what was to become his lifelong passion: photography.

As is the case with many young people, his life was interrupted by unexpected circumstances. This interruption came when the Civil War broke out in 1861. Although he was only sixteen years old at the time, he tried to enlist in the army but was rejected because of his age. His motivation for wanting to join was not so much patriotic as it was practical. In the army, he would have food and shelter, luxuries that were sorely lacking in his civilian life. Finally, at age seventeen, he was able to join Company E, Sixteenth Ohio Volunteer Infantry, in Millersburg, where he served for about three years. Although he was underage, he was accepted on the strength of a letter written by his mother giving her permission. There is some skepticism about the authenticity of the letter.

At a skirmish at Cumberland Gap, Ted was taken prisoner but was released nine days later in a prisoner exchange agreement between the two armies. Even in prison, he was grateful for what he had. He extolled the generosity of one of his captors who gave him a loaf of bread during his incarceration. To Ted, even a loaf of bread was a luxury.

Continuing with his not-so-picture-perfect life, Ted contracted malaria while in the army and was a victim of an explosion that injured his head, causing all the hair on one side to fall out. When he saw his mother sometime later, he tried to shelter her from the shock of the injury on his head, so he told her not to hug him because he was infested with lice. The record shows that this excuse was for naught; his mother did not heed his warning and hugged him anyway. She, too, had never recovered from the separation, and seeing her son alive following the war was a blessing she never expected.

Following his honorable discharge, Ted intended to become a civil engineer, but he needed more education to be accepted for such a challenging course of study. He could not afford more education, so he came to Wadsworth to start a photography studio, borrowing $200 to do so, an astronomical amount to a poor lad who had nothing from the beginning. He took the plunge and, with dogged conservatism, was able to pay off the debt before it was due, therein saving fifty cents in interest payments.

Ted married Alice Rothacker of Doylestown in 1871, and they had a son. These events were the high points of his otherwise struggling existence. Unfortunately, the joy was only temporary. In 1898, their son died at age twenty-six, throwing Ted into a round of depression that surpassed all the other grief and sorrow he had experienced from birth. He and Alice never recovered from this loss, despite the support of a community that now had elevated them to "honored citizens" status for all their involvement in and contributions to their adopted village.

So widespread was the regard the community had for their "photographer" that, on the occasion of Ted and Alice's fiftieth wedding anniversary in February 1921, committees from the various lodges in Wadsworth arranged a reception in the couple's honor, an event that was hosted in the Independent Order of Odd Fellows (IOOF) building on Main Street. Several hundred

The Wolbach home on High Street served as Ted's studio until he died. Other photographers occupied the house as well in later years.

people attended the gala. In Ted's and Alice's minds, everyone was there except for one person: their son.

Only storybooks relate coincidences that equaled the experience Ted had while in the army. A shell exploded near the tent where Ted and his tent mate were sleeping, killing his partner. In an act of charity, he took the personal effects from the dead body beside him and found a picture of a girl in the pocket. Much to his surprise, Ted recognized the photo as being one he had made while working at the Wooster gallery. The tent mate had never mentioned anything about the girl, so Ted did not know her name. He made an exhaustive search for her when he returned home but did not find her until she was very old and with impaired memory.

Ted never forgot his father. Even twenty-two years after his father's death, Ted felt the need to be close to his father and went to Toledo to claim his remains. He brought them back to Wadsworth and kept the precious

Theodore Wolbach photographed most of Wadsworth during his tenure as a photographer. The negative of his own life was developed as he became one of Wadsworth's most influential citizens.

remembrance—now nothing but dust—in his photography studio for eighteen years. When his mother died in 1894, Ted buried both of them at Woodlawn Cemetery. He buried both people who gave him life but could not bury the memories.

Photography was his occupation, passion and art; community service was his vocation. Ted was a councilman, a member of the board of education, a devout and active Lutheran, a member of several civic organizations and the ninth mayor of Wadsworth. In addition, he was a leader in the Grand Army of the Republic (GAR) and a captain in the National Guard. He was renowned for his ironclad memory, and people would depend on him to remember various incidents that occurred. He always did so with accuracy, probably because he had photographed the people or the event.

Theodore Wolbach's almost endless supply of pictures was displayed in the old Wadsworth Library in the room behind where the books were housed. When the new library was built to replace the original Leiter House Library, a decision was made to move the Wolbach collection to the Medina County Historical Society Museum, where it resides today.

Theodore Wolbach was a man born into poverty who lived in poverty, survived poverty and conquered poverty. He was a man who gave all he had and who left all he had. At the end, he had it all—all but what he wanted most: a complete family and the grandchildren who were never to be.

For us today, he is a man who lives through his pictures.

PART II

THE SOUTH END

Without It, Wadsworth Might Have Gone "South"

The South End of Wadsworth is usually written with capital letters since historically the rest of the community has regarded it as a less desirable region of Wadsworth rather than a direction from the square. Actually, the South End was once a thriving community that housed Wadsworth's most prominent and professional citizens.

These people either were themselves or produced some of the most recognizable leaders in Wadsworth who led the village (and later the city) in government, commerce, industry and education. It is assumed that many of the early residents moved to the northern part of the community after the railroad went through, since the wind would blow smoke over their homes in the South End.

The railroad was supposed to go through Doylestown but came through Wadsworth instead because the grade going into Doylestown was too steep for the trains of the day. Despite the fact that the present grade—seven miles east from the Silvercreek crossing and seven miles west—is the longest grade between New York and Chicago on the Erie tracks, it was routed through the South End because the grade through that part of the village was more gradual than the one going into Doylestown or anywhere else in Wadsworth.

The original train station was made of old boxcars that were salvaged from previous train mishaps. It was replaced by a station that was torn down several years ago.

Had the railroad not been routed through Wadsworth, perhaps Wadsworth would have never grown as it did. It could, indeed, have gone "south." Because of the railroad, however, industries developed nearby so that they could use the more economical and farther-reaching mode of transportation—rails—to carry their goods throughout the nation.

With industries locating in the South End, the value of residential homes declined, and the original "originals"—community leaders, professional people and those with means—moved northward in large numbers. The decreased value made the area homes affordable for the working class, and as a result, the South End became a blue-collar mecca. It became known as a less desirable section of town in which to live. During World War II, people migrating from the southern states to work in Wadsworth's plants began to congregate in the South End as well. The blue-collar progeny of the European "originals" began improving themselves through education and ambition, and they, too, moved to other parts of Wadsworth, where at one time they had been discouraged from living.

In the latter part of the twentieth century, the boundaries of the southern sector of the Wadsworth community began expanding farther south, edging on Johnson Road, about a mile from what had been the accepted boundary line. These new modern and upscale houses attracted families who were employed in business and professional venues. The present demographics do not resemble the array of nationalities that the South End once embraced or the political persuasions once espoused. For years, Ward 3 was considered the only Democratic stronghold in the city; today, this is no longer true.

The original blue-collar ethnic community in the South End produced at least ten college professors; three university deans; at least four published scholars; at least two judges; several lawyers; at least one bank president; physicians; a trucking giant; many teachers; ministers of various denominations; scientists; at least one medical researcher; several business owners; at least one pharmaceutical giant; the father of Wadsworth's only native astronaut, Michael Foreman (Wadsworth has two other ties to astronauts: Steve Smith, son-in-law of Pat and Joan Brannigan, and Michael Good, son of former Wadsworthite Bob Good, son of Don and Kathleen Koehler Good); at least three widely known professional musicians; and countless other professional, mechanical and worthy citizens of Wadsworth.

Perhaps the capital letters should finally be removed so that the designation "south end" signifies direction rather than socioeconomics.

George Wise

Who Was He?

One of the first industries to develop in the South End was the Wise and Loomis Wadsworth Machine Company, located on Mechanic Street immediately adjacent to the railroad. Among other products, it manufactured farm equipment, making Wadsworth a major center for producing wagons, sleds and other implements for agricultural use.

George Wise was a partner of Erastus Loomis, whose biography appeared in *Remembering Wadsworth: From Pioneers to Streetcars*, but snippets of his life will be repeated here to support the contributions he and George made to the South End.

Erastus was the person to "discover" coal lying on the ground in Silvercreek while he was cutting timbers in the heavily forested far-southeast section of the village. By mining the coal and owning the first mines, he became wealthy and built the first three-story building in Medina County (the Odd Fellows Hall on Main Street). He reputedly underwrote the cost of the Union School, built many houses and owned huge acreages of woods in Michigan and Missouri, among other things. His many enterprises were so numerous that he could no longer administer all of them.

In 1863, Loomis approached George Wise to become a partner in what had been family-owned endeavors. There is no documentation as to why George was chosen to become a partner with a family that owned so much. It can only be assumed they had extraordinary confidence in George since there is no evidence George had capital to contribute to the partnership.

When Erastus's brother, Edgar, died in 1870, Erastus and George continued the operations as Wise and Loomis. George Wise was sent

Early workers at the Garfield Injector. The factory was named for President Garfield, a frequent visitor to his friend Burke Hinsdale's home. Hinsdale succeeded Garfield as president of Hiram College after Garfield became president of the United States.

to administer the lumber acreages and, while doing so, built a small empire of lumber mills and shingle-making mills, employing a total of 180 people combined.

Not satisfied with working only with lumber, coal and real estate, Wise built a machine shop on Mechanics Street that started out making farm machinery. Although Akron had the reputation for being the center for the manufacture of farm implements, there is support for the notion that the genesis was in south Wadsworth under the aegis of the Youngs and George Wise.

Wise and Loomis (note the order of names, despite Wise coming in as a late "partner") wielded significant influence in the expansion of Wadsworth from a pioneer town into one that was rapidly becoming industrial. His "machine shop" later became the home of Garfield Injector, a forerunner of the Ohio Injector Company.

Coal mining entered oblivion in the mid-1930s, but forward-thinking Wise, as well as countless others, ignited the spark that laid the foundation for industrial Wadsworth. There is an eerie coincidence that the farm on which coal was originally found was the Wise Farm. There appears to be no documentation to tie the two Wise families together, but it is possible that there is a relationship and that therein lies the genesis of the Wise-Loomis partnership.

Dr. Hanson Hard

An Early Couch Potato

Although it is all but forgotten, Wadsworth was the center for an innovation that put people on restful and comfortable beds, as well as in soft chairs and couches. Dr. Hanson, Elbert and Pulaski Hard, William Eyles (who married into the Hard/Pardee families), William Freeborn and D.S. Greenwald had at least one of the three factories that made the new spiral springs for beds, chairs and sofas. They had a patented method of affixing these springs to the frame that, once again, had the rest of the nation pointing to Wadsworth as a force to observe—all in the South End. Before coil springs were manufactured in 1865, beds and furniture were cushioned with wool, straw or feathers.

Not much is written about Dr. Hanson Hard except that he was one of five doctors who was educated at Dr. George Pardee's Medical School. As is indicated throughout Wadsworth's early history, medical students "read medicine," meaning they were apprentices under a master doctor, much the same as some craftsmen are today.

The Hard family was prominent in Wadsworth, and it is no coincidence Hanson was a student of Dr. George Pardee, since they were related in a manner of speaking. Julia Hard was the first wife of Don Pardee, and Caroline Hard was the wife of George Pardee. In fact, there were so many cousins in the Pardee, Hard and Eyles families that, had they not been residents of Wadsworth, the population of the village would have been diminished substantially. Nonetheless, the Pardee, Hard and Eyles families all distinguished themselves as community leaders, politicians, mayors, doctors, dentists, attorneys and business owners.

Elbert and Pulaski Hard were not medical students but had ingenious ideas that came from Dr. Hanson's involvement in medicine. Hanson contended, "One of the perennial discomforts of humankind is the misalignment of body geometry." If all the bones, muscles and whatever else makes up the body are in alignment with one another, the body has few or no aches and pains. If not, the body aches and requires management. In those days, there was little medication to alleviate infirmity. Enter Dr. Hanson, who knew how to manage the pain. He would place the patient in a restful position, and the body's system would heal itself. Dr. Hanson presented the data; Elbert and Pulaski devised the solution. (As a note of interest, Pulaski was named for General Casimir Pulaski, the Polish patriot who became a soldier of fortune in the Revolutionary War and saved the life of General George Washington. He was then made a general of the army but died of wounds suffered at the Battle of Savannah. He is only one of seven people ever to be awarded honorary citizenship to the United States.)

Some of the stories that surrounded the medical schools in Wadsworth were not at all what today's public relations firms would use as promotional material. There are stories about the medical school students having to dig up bodies to use in the study of human anatomy. Whether this was fact or rumor, it was, nevertheless, the news on the streets. What *would* have been good material for a public relations campaign was Dr. Hanson's work in alleviating sore backs and muscles: "Dr. Hanson Hard Working with Brothers to Alleviate Pain." This headline did not make the news, probably because it did not have the macabre intrigue of digging up bodies.

Pulaski Hard was of particular value in that he was an attorney. Before he became involved with the coil spring enterprise, he practiced law and was quite successful both in Wadsworth and in Summit County. Pulaski's strength in the newly formed company, however, came from the fact that he was the station agent for the Atlantic and Great Western Railroad from 1865 to 1872. This position was of great importance since this was the beginning of railroads and only select people could qualify as agents. The agent not only involved himself with normal day-to-day activities but also was heavily involved with legal issues, such as land acquisition, tariff questions, interstate travel and law and tort issues that surfaced when the railroad went through private property. Hard's knowledge of the process and the contacts he gained through these endeavors gave him an advantage when trying to open doors to garner acceptance for the coil spring patent. Getting a patent in the mid-1800s was a daunting task; the Industrial Revolution was just beginning, and there were throngs of people surfacing with various inventions. The details of the Hard family getting the patent will not be presented here, but they are of some consequence, even though we take coil springs for granted today.

The Hunsbergers, Kulp and Nash

Added Utility to Comfort

One industry begets another. Just a few hundred feet away from the coil spring factory, the Reverend Mr. Ephriam Hunsberger, J.G. Kulp, Samuel Nash and Christian Hunsberger built a sawmill that made doors, sashes and window shades. The room was now complete: Wadsworth Machine Company made springs for beds, chairs and sofas, and its neighbor made products to make the room looked finished.

The Pennsylvania Dutch were generally farmers, but some ventured away from the farm to ply other crafts at which they were masters: woodworking and carpentry.

Although Ephriam Hunsberger was a minister and brought the First Mennonite Church to Wadsworth, he had to make a living outside the pulpit since Mennonite preachers did not receive pay in those days. Ephriam, J.G. Kulp, Sam Nash and Christian Hunsberger (never called anything but Christian to preserve the significance of the name) were all of Pennsylvania

Ephriam Hunsberger not only brought the First Mennonite Church to Wadsworth but also became a key figure in manufacturing.

Dutch heritage, with the same strong work ethic, honesty and values usually attributed to the Pennsylvania Dutch. The fact that the Pennsylvania Dutch became leaders in industry is not surprising in that their numbers surpassed the numbers of the original English by four to one just forty years after they first arrived from Pennsylvania.

Each of the men had experience in either furniture making or building. Wadsworth was a natural for anything wooden, since there were vast acreages of timber in the region, especially in the Silvercreek area. Oak, maple, ash, hickory, walnut, birch and just about any other hardwood were within easy reach. The Kulp-Nash-Hunsberger team used nothing but hardwood to make doors and sashes. Window shades were often made of wooden slats, much the same as venetian blinds are today; however, windows not covered by drapes or shades made of cloth were covered with shutters, also made in the new factory.

There are accounts of these men sawing the timber in Silvercreek and transporting the logs along the railroad tracks to the mill. There are even some references to their having either built or bought a handcar to ride the rails to their mill. (A handcar is a vehicle that rides on the rails but is propelled by one or two men pumping handles to activate the wheels. Later, they became motorized.) There is no written documentation regarding this, but descendants of the early families remember tales about such practices. In some accounts, there are even descriptions about dumping the logs off the handcar and letting them roll down the hill from the tracks close to where the mill was located. This is believable since there is documentation that when the village built the sidewalks on Injector Hill, logs were rolled to the bottom of the hill from the railroad tracks and cut into slats at that point. After sawing them to appropriate lengths and widths, the slats were nailed to the timbers that served as the base for the sidewalks.

Others Who Contributed to the South End Industrial Incubator

The Match Shop was born after 1890. On the site that would later become the Ohio Match Company, Abraham Yoder built another sash and door company, since the first company could not supply enough of its products fast enough to satisfy the appetites of the growing customer base.

The Ohio Injector moved the Garfield Injector Company from Mechanic Street (adjacent to the railroad) to its present location, where it has remained for well over one hundred years, although under different names. But before the Garfield Injector moved there, Cyrus Hard founded the Wadsworth Woolen Mill on that location to expand what he was doing on a smaller scale elsewhere in Wadsworth. He moved his cottage industry to an industrial height simply because he wanted to be close to the railroad to ship his goods far and wide. He later sold it to Robert Aspinall and Hiram Yockey in 1875. They carded wool mechanically—a departure from hand carding—from sheep raised throughout the community. They processed the wool and sold it for use in clothing or for anything else that used wool in its production, such as mattresses and pillows.

Many years later, when the Ohio companies were in full bloom, grocery stores, cafés, saloons, clothing stores, hardware stores, barbershops, filling stations, candy stores, restaurants, lumber mills, gristmills, feed stores, fishnet manufacturing, coal yards and drugstores flourished in the South End. Notable among the grocery stores were Fenton and Leatherman, DiPolito's Market, Heighberger's Grocery, Chuppa's Grocery and Momchilov's Grocery. Other stores included Bacso Hardware; Bacso Clothing; Eckhoff Echo Grill; various saloons; Police's Barbershop; Dudas' Barbershop; Freeman Drug; Norm Boyer's filling station; Barras Birkbeck's (candy and sundries); Sticher's Restaurant; Dutt, Holvey and Lesher (DH&L mill and feed); Bacso Coal Yard and others.

The South End had some of the most spectacular fires in Wadsworth's history. The Wadsworth Salt Company (not to be confused with the Ohio Salt Company) burned to the ground in October 1928. Another spectacular fire erupted on October 31, 1997, when an arsonist torched Wadsworth Sash and Door in the South End and Holmesbrook Lumber Company at the same time. Bill Stewart, owner of Sash and Door, and Holmesbrook owners, Tom and Steve Hudson, suffered immense losses given the enormity of the fires and despite the twenty-four fire companies that gave the Wadsworth Fire Department assistance to extinguish the infernos.

FIRE CHIEF HARRISON G. SEARS

Fighting Hell with a Squirt Gun

When the Wadsworth Salt Company burned, the flames shot so high they could be seen from all the outlying areas of Wadsworth. Firefighting equipment in those days was minimal at best, and the possibility of saving the building was almost nonexistent given the intensity of the blaze. The origin of the fire was never determined.

Harrison G. Sears was the fire chief for this fire. In fact, by virtue of Wadsworth becoming a city in 1931, he was the first fire chief, appointed by then mayor L.S. Wertz, of Wertz Buggy fame. All others who preceded him had been fire marshals.

However minimal the structure of the department, when Sears took the helm, he felt the necessity to divide the fire department into two units: the hook-and-ladder company and the engine company. The ladder for the hook-and-ladder company was forty feet long. The engine had an eighty-gallon capacity with two hundred feet of hose. This equipment cost $800 when it was purchased in 1903. Needless to say, such minimal firefighting equipment was insufficient for nearly any fire, much less for one the size of that which consumed large buildings.

Sears joined the department as a volunteer in 1898 (some accounts say 1900) and was one of the organizers of volunteer firemen. He had no intention of becoming chief; he merely wanted to serve. Nonetheless, he became chief in 1900 and remained with the department for thirty-five years. He fought fires almost until the time of his death.

Early firefighting in Wadsworth depended more on human resources than on equipment. More sophisticated equipment did not appear until the early 1920s.

Although the equipment used then was "prehistoric" by today's standards, Sears had walked his way through an era that was truly primitive. He started with the bucket brigade, advanced to a tiny hand-drawn chemical cart and then worked a pump that Andy Auble attached to one of his old automobiles. The reader should remember that Andy Auble had the first automobile in Wadsworth, and in the very early days of the century, an "old" car was not too terribly old—nor powerful—but it was powerful enough to pull a small pump to fires.

By the time the Salt Company fire erupted, Chief Sears had moved the equipment of the fire department into the twentieth century. He had a fire truck with high-pressure water pumps and an extension ladder that purchased in 1925. Despite this "modern" equipment, the Salt Company burned to the ground with no hope of salvaging any part of it. What remained was a pile of rubble.

Harry Sears was a strong man, a personification of Henry Wadsworth Longfellow's blacksmith poem:

Under a spreading chestnut-tree, The village smithy stands;
The smith, a mighty man is he, With large and sinewy hands;
And the muscles of his brawny arms are strong as iron bands.

A blacksmith by trade, Harry was a fierce proponent of physical fitness. He instituted the four-mile sprint for all volunteer firemen. This tactic was legendary in Wadsworth, and only the fittest could survive. Men would don what resembled bathing suits and run four miles on regular intervals. Those who were not able to endure the pace could not continue as firemen. Harry's rationale was simple: firemen had to be strong to pull the equipment, pump water by hand and lift heavy girders and fit enough to run out of a building if the fire became too hot. Running the four miles, he contended, also increased the breathing power of the fireman so he could hold his breath while inside a burning building. Running increased leg muscles as well, so climbing a ladder with a load—either a hose or a person—would be less of a challenge.

A competitor of sorts, Harry entered firemen into various endurance contests: carrying hoses up ladders in a given span of seconds, carrying a person a long distance, lifting heavy objects and anything else that would increase physical strength. His men walked away with top honors each time

Harrison Sears was the first fire chief in Wadsworth and brought the fire department into the twentieth century as well as he could given the budding technology that existed at the time. *Courtesy Wadsworth Fire Department.*

they competed. Harry believed that the competitions gave the men cause and motivation to endure the arduous and monotonous four-mile runs.

Not to be outdone by any of his firemen, Harry ran with the volunteers and did so to the end. He was also the night watchman for the village until two policemen were hired to patrol the streets in 1932. He was a blacksmith in town for forty-two years, building his upper body muscles by swinging heavy sledges. Those who knew Harry said the villagers respected him not only for his strength but also for his dedication to firefighting and to the community.

THE MATCH SHOP WOMEN

Liberated by the Match Before Women's Lib

During the growth cycle of the industries, the South End was a center for women in the workplace, almost exclusively at the Match. The Match gave women a liberation they had never felt before, since the only previous occupations for women were confined to domestic labor in the nonprofessional arena and secretarial work or teaching and nursing in the commercial or professional fields. Even in teaching, men dominated.

Not only did women work at the Match as employees, but they played and socialized there as well. The "Match Girls" were a formidable group when placed on the basketball court. The Match actually built a gym for the express purpose of giving employees a place to exercise and participate in family events. The surprising issue here is that women appeared to use the gym more than men and were encouraged to do so by management.

According to *Match Tips*, the house organ for the Match, women did not begin to become "family" (or organized) until the Match had been in operation for a number of years. Names of female leaders are not mentioned in *Match Tips*. Reference is made only to their activities and not to any underlying strategy to organize. But organize they did.

With a ratio of three men to every woman, men still dominated. Notwithstanding the three-to-one ratio, the women made their voices heard, and their zeal was unrelenting. While men made between five and nine cents per hour in the early 1900s, women made even less. The Match Girls began talking with one another, and before long, they had a modicum of strength.

The Match Girls, shown as they were required to dress in the early days. Although many women worked at the Match, they were outnumbered four to one by men.

What started as small gatherings escalated into "teams." There are those who think there was an underlying motivation not only for camaraderie but for economic purposes as well. Camaraderie prevailed; the economics thrust did not fare nearly so well, but it did improve. After much time had elapsed, the social and athletic enthusiasm brought many women together who would never have had an opportunity for competitive sports. It also provided them with one of the first forums in which they could combine their individual strengths into a cooperative force—all in the Match Shop gym.

William E. Artman

He Opened Many "Valves" in Wadsworth

The Young family deserves the distinction of being the fathers of the Ohio companies—Ohio Injector, Ohio Match, Ohio Salt and Ohio Boxboard. Grandiose credit is due them for their pioneer spirit and industrial initiatives.

Wadsworth will be forever beholden to them for their contribution to the livelihood of the hundreds of families they supported through employment and their vast philanthropic gifts to the community.

Their unparalleled growth can be attributed to their keen business and mechanical ingenuity, as well as to their administrative strategy to surround themselves with skilled people while always maintaining control of the direction they wanted their companies to go.

One of these skilled people was William E. Artman, a man who came to Wadsworth when he was a full-grown adult. Bill started his life in Northumberland County, Pennsylvania, in 1852, and in 1864, when he was twelve, he left home to explore the possibilities of what the world had to offer.

One of the popular occupations of the day was telegraphy, since it was used almost exclusively for communicating before the telephone overtook it. Learning this trade was relatively simple: one merely had to learn the dots-and-dashes equivalents for twenty-six letters and then learn how to use the relatively simple equipment. What was more difficult was trying to find an employer that needed these kinds of skills, since there were so many flooding the field. Bill's superior skills boded well for him to find a position with the railroad system, where he worked for about fifteen years as a telegrapher and then as a station manager.

Bill had many contacts as a station manager and heard about the Young family and their Garfield Injector, then located across the tracks from the Wadsworth depot on Mechanic Street. This renovated railroad car structure was not only the center for railroad communications but also a gathering place for railroad people, local merchants and the public in general. It is not known whether Bill learned about the Garfield Injector in the depot or whether he heard about it from other sources; nonetheless, he was aware of it.

Bill was quick to make contact with the Young family and invested some money in what was then a budding industry. His experience as a stationmaster and his own drive to become successful proved beneficial to him, as well as to the new company. Within a short time, he became the secretary-treasurer of the Garfield Injector and then was involved in details of the formation of the Ohio Match Company, the Ohio Salt and the Ohio Boxboard. Bill was associated with much of the early success of the new companies, given his managerial skills and indefatigable drive.

William Artman, the man who is credited for telephone, water, electric and sewer services in Wadsworth. E.J. Young is on the right.

The powerhouse with the water tank next to it. The building still stands at 365 Broad Street, but the water tank was demolished several years ago.

Baited with the success he had gained as an industrialist and recognizing the need for the new power that was coming into its own (electric), he started the Wadsworth Light and Water Company, a private organization that the city later purchased and operated as a public service.

Telephones were also becoming more than a novelty and "toy" for the avant-garde "tekkies," as we would call them today. Wadsworth was without a strong base for telephone communication, although there were some telephones in town, so Bill organized the Wadsworth Telephone Company, the forerunner of the various companies that succeeded it (the Star Telephone Company, the Northern Ohio Telephone Company and others). Artman's venture expanded the horizons of telephone communication in Wadsworth by making the telephone available to the masses rather than to just a few. People could now talk with one another in the village or in their neighborhood, not just to people in other communities where a telephone might exist.

Although Bill was not a native of Wadsworth, he married into one of the early settler families when he took Lydia Sours Kremer as his wife. John and Lydia Kremer, Lydia's parents, were charter members of the Trinity Reformed Church (now the United Church of Christ), making them pioneers twice—once when they came to Wadsworth during the early

Early telephone operators needed to be dexterous, agile and mechanically inclined to connect one caller to the other.

days of settlement and again when they were among the organizers of the Reformed Church.

Bill's interests and contributions were not limited to industry alone. He was recognized in another venue as well—education—when he was elected to the board of education in Wadsworth and was appointed a member of the board of regents of Heidelberg College at Tiffin, Ohio, one of the church schools of the Reformed Church. Even the village sought out his services: he was appointed to the cemetery board to help with the expansion of the then small burial ground. Much land was acquired, fitted, drained and reconfigured for cemetery use during his tenure and beyond, the outcome of which is the present cemetery that reaches from West Street to Beck Street and from College Street to beyond Baldwin Street—this from only a small plat donated by Frederick Brown many years earlier.

In 1903, Bill, the newcomer-turned-industrialist, built a huge house on the top of Injector Hill. Although it was an impressive dwelling, the design of the house is not so noteworthy. What *is* noteworthy is where he built it: on the fringe of the area that would be served by a "sewer" system that would have its birth in 1907, a vision Bill nurtured and worked to achieve. Since Bill was on the committee to establish the system, he knew where it would end, and he wanted his house to be on the system. The house was razed many years ago; only an expanse of grass is there now.

The Garfield Injector, the Ohio Injector, the Ohio Match, the Ohio Boxboard and the Ohio Salt were all companies that supported the Wadsworth economy for years, with William Artman as one of the important players. In addition, the Wadsworth Light and Water, the Wadsworth Telephone

The Garfield Injector Company became the Ohio Injector Company, moved from Mechanics Street to Main Street and actually had an office building, shown here.

Company and a sewer system were infant entities destined to become the behemoths upon which we anchor our lives today.

Despite all these achievements, William Artman's name rarely comes up in conversation when we talk about Wadsworth history; however, at one time this was not the case. After his death in 1928, a monument was erected in his honor in Woodlawn Cemetery. The monument weighs 14.5 tons and is placed on a 5.5-ton base. It is carved out of the finest Barre, Vermont granite and is known to have no imperfections. This was the regard Wadsworth had for William Artman.

The original generation that recognized him as one of Wadsworth's energetic and forward-thinking citizens is now gone. Replacing it is the present generation, whose memories are also fading. The future generation will probably not even whisper his name as time goes on, but the monument in the cemetery and this account of William Artman will serve to give meaning to a name we should remember every time we pick up a telephone, turn on a light, flush a toilet or drink from a faucet.

Bill's hand touched them all.

The Good Folks at the Wadsworth Salvation Army

Wadsworth has always been involved with agriculture or industry. The major industries started in the 1890s with the Garfield Injector (later Ohio Injector), Ohio Match, Ohio Boxboard and Wadsworth Salt as the largest industries. Later, some smaller industries came to Wadsworth, specifically the Kemetex Company (made window shades), the Exel Tire and Rubber, the Wadsworth Foundry and the brickyard.

When the economy was good, smoke bellowed from the chimneys. When work was slow, the smoke disappeared. To some—especially innocent children—no smoke meant no smells. One little boy told his father he was glad the smell was gone. His father told him, "If you don't smell the smoke, your daddy don't work and you don't eat."

Cycles of lack of work meant people were, indeed, not eating. Enter the Salvation Army from Barberton, Ohio. Since Wadsworth didn't have a Salvation Army in the early days of the century, it depended on Barberton for charitable aid. This was better than no aid, but Barberton had its own problems and could not support two communities that had the same industrial footprint. Both were idle at the same time.

In 1923, the General Headquarters of the International Salvation Army established a separate unit of the Salvation Army in Wadsworth and appointed Captain Ralph Phillips as commander. The location was where the need was: close to the factories that supported people in good times and where people needed support in bad.

Lieutenant Watson Hoffman came on board to assist Captain Phillips in January 1924. In May, he was promoted to captain and replaced Captain Phillips. Captain Hoffman had a brother, Captain Paul, who replaced him in 1928. With the Depression on the cusp of whirling across the national landscape in 1929, Captain Hoffman had more than he felt he could handle. Adding to this was the birth of his son, Peter, in 1930. A new father, a new captain, a new commander of the Salvation Army, a new Depression—all of these taxed the strength and resources of this new leader. Captain Hoffman called on the Lord and the people of Wadsworth for continued support. Soon, the entire city was in a state of financial and emotional depression, and many, many more came to Captain Hoffman for assistance.

Starting its service in Wadsworth in a tiny building on the northwest corner of State and Main Streets, the Salvation Army began sustaining the needy, despite the strain of having to maintain its own needs, even these minimal quarters. Contributions to assist the Salvation Army were nonexistent or meager at best. People did not have pennies to give but gave them anyway. The accommodations were not large enough for the expanding needs of the Salvation Army, forcing it to move to a larger facility. In 1928, despite having inadequate funding, it moved to the east side of Main Street. Again, this space was already too small for efficient operations, but it was what was affordable and available for little or no cost.

In 1934, major contributions from seven people from Wadsworth, as well as pennies and extra change collected from many other individuals, allowed the Salvation Army to purchase the brick building north of the original quarters. This building was considerably larger than the previous two put together, a real advantage since 1934 found Wadsworth at the height of the Great Depression, forcing the Salvation Army to expand the scope of its programs to serve the growing needs of the community.

One program was designed to bring young people, children and their families together for recreation. Movies were in their infancy at that time, but there were "talkies" already gracing the silver screens across the nation. The Wadsworth Salvation Army did not have a silver screen; instead, it used the side of the lumber company storage shed to flash the light beam from the less-than-state-of-the-art projector. Viewers sat on the ground or brought chairs for additional comfort.

Soup lines in the 1930s were long, as was the list of needs for the poor. The Great Depression continued to claim more victims, resulting in hordes of people becoming more dependent on food charity to exist. They found what would sustain them in the daily soup kitchens provided by the Salvation Army. The soup kitchen fare was just that: soup made in the Salvation Army kitchen by volunteers.

Serving the ever-growing numbers of needy became more than even the new quarters could accommodate, so the Salvation Army had to improvise. It used the outside of the lumber shed for picture shows and the inside to house the soup kitchen. Scores of people would gather inside the mill room every day to accept the blessing of another meal.

In an interview with Captain Paul's son, Peter, in 2007, he shared that Captain Paul and his family worked night and day to beg for food for the needy. They relied heavily on farmers, who would give them vegetables and, on occasion, meat during butchering season.

Captain Paul believed the people needed more than food, outdoor movies and coal. A musician himself, he organized a band that played on the streets, especially during the Christmas season around the kettles. Captain Paul recruited these players from people who came to the Salvation Army for food, clothing or other assistance. Those few who volunteered received the very best instruction he could offer at no charge. There are stories about some of these students going on to become distinguished musicians, an advantage they would have never had without the instruction they received from Captain Paul in those early days.

When kettles were placed on the streets between Thanksgiving and Christmas, players would be there to accompany them. Nonplayers would ring the bells, and the three or four musicians would play Christmas carols. Crowds would gather around to listen to the harmonizing strains of the carols from the somewhat unbalanced instrumentation assembled and would give their contributions in blessings since they had no money to offer.

Older Wadsworth residents remember the Salvation Army Band playing in front of the Citizens Bank building, dressed in full attire and pretending not to be cold. They remember the frozen brass instruments and struggling fingers moving painfully to force tones that would glorify their efforts. They remember the occasional clink of a coin that would drop into the kettle and the tear that would run down the cheek of the lady cornet player when it happened.

There is an old saying: flies land even on the tired horse. After suffering through many years of opprobrious times, the Salvation Army building caught fire in 1944 and its contents and inner structure were destroyed. Money was scarce, the Salvation Army had just squeezed through the Great Depression, it was strapped for personnel with World War II taking its officers and volunteers for service to the military and insurance did not cover the cost of the loss. Yet, it recovered. It cost $3,000 more to rebuild the structure than the insurance offered. Despite all this, the Salvation Army not only rebuilt the structure to its original utility, but it also dug out the basement—with donated hand labor—and outfitted it with tools and machinery for the boys' club and the Salvation Army Boy Scout troop.

Today, some of our erstwhile citizens, past and present civic leaders, industrial and professional greats and countless other nameless people are here because of the sustenance they received from the Salvation Army in Wadsworth during those tempestuous times of deprivation and need. Their gratitude is great, but it never surpasses the generosity of this institution for which there has always been a need and always will be.

The following are personal accounts of people who were helped by the Wadsworth Salvation Army and later became leaders in the community. Names have been changed to preserve the identity of those interviewed.

> *Sally: There were six of us. My dad was an alcoholic and wasn't working. My mother had no skills and no education. We were starving. We went to the Salvation Army in the South End, and they let us have one meal a day at the lumberyard. I thank God every day for the Army. Today I am able to give back to them for all they did for us. If it hadn't been for the army, I wouldn't be here today.* [Sally is a retired community leader.]

> *Sherman: My parents were quite well off when we were younger, but when the Depression hit, my father lost everything he had, and we had nothing to eat. I remember the handouts the Army gave us in the early '30s and*

watching the movies on the side of the lumberyard building. [Sherman became a high finance executive.]

Addie: My parents were born in Europe and came to this country during the Depression. The Match wasn't working every day, and we had it tough. Although we were Catholic, the Salvation Army gave us food and some clothes. I still have a little dress they gave us. I will never give it up because it reminds me of how happy I was when I got to wear it to school rather than the rag I had been wearing. [Annie married well and is a surviving widow of a repair garage owner. She volunteers for the charitable organizations in retirement.]

Sara: My dad was out of work and our family was starving. It made him mad and sad at the same time, but that didn't help. He would get so mad, sometimes he would take it out on us kids. My mom couldn't take it any more so she went to the Salvation Army, and the captain there—I don't remember his name—was so kind to her, he told her to bring the family that night and get some soup. My dad didn't want to go at first, but then he did, and we ate for the first time in days. After that we went on a regular basis. [Sara became a majorette in high school and later became a teacher. In her retirement, she volunteers for the Salvation Army any time she can.]

Steve: My sister and I went to Lincoln School one day, and the teacher noticed we didn't bring any lunch. She went to the office and told the principal. He came and got us and asked if we were hungry. We both said we were, so he took us down to a building on Main Street and someone gave us something to eat. I later learned it was the Salvation Army. When we got home, we told our mom and she started to cry. My dad was outside, and when he came in, she told him. He told my mom that maybe its time we swallowed our pride and went to the soup line. We did this almost every night for a long time. [Steve moved to Chicago after high school and, with persistence, worked himself to the presidency of a small company. He contributes money every Christmas to the Salvation Army.]

There are many stories such as the ones cited above. People from all walks of life credit the Salvation Army for helping them through a difficult period, making it possible for them to become what they are today.

The Salvation Army has since moved again. As was the case in the past, and will probably be again in the future, the quarters are not sufficient for its needs. The Salvation Army, however, will prevail.

It always has.

HIRAM YOCKEY AND THE MEN WHO BUILT THE BRICKYARD

Follow the Red Brick Road Around the World

The name of the place where bricks were made in Wadsworth was never uttered without the word *the* preceding it, as in "the Brickyard." Yet that was never the name of the firm whose bricks have enhanced the beauty and added stability to buildings throughout the world, including Fort Knox, the Ford plant in Detroit and probably anywhere else where a brick edifice is located.

An early brickyard. Bricks shown were used essentially for paving and, in some cases, buildings such as that in the picture.

Residents of Wadsworth today know that the brickyard is located on nearly three hundred acres of land south of the city. It didn't start there. In fact, it started many other places in Wadsworth and finally ended up there.

Hiram Yockey, one of Wadsworth's earlier residents and the son of one of the founders of the German Reformed Church (now the United Church of Christ), fired his first kiln in Silvercreek on a piece of land that would later become known as the Yockey Farm. The reason for choosing this location, so it was thought at the time, was that there was good clay there and it was close to the railroad.

The Connecticut Western Reserve was divided into sections of about 640 acres. One such section was one mile east of what is now the center of town (the real center was to have been where Isham School is located, but for a variety of reasons it was not placed there), extending south one mile, bordered by Durling Drive, Silver Crest Road, Silvercreek Road and Broad Street. The Yockey kilns were in the southeast portion of that section, on a quarter section (160 acres) about one thousand feet north of the railroad tracks.

According to the old-time farmers—now all deceased—the reason the kilns didn't prosper was because the land was so rich it needed to be used for farming and certainly not for firing bricks. As a result, the section was transformed into farmland, and in 1893, the Yockey family built their barn there, established their residence and began farming.

Bricks then were produced at the end of Chestnut Street, again within easy reach of the railroad, and soon, brick houses appeared on Wadsworth streets. Seeing the prospects of a market for bricks, another kiln was established at Clark's Corners near a spur of the old coal-mining track that led to the main tracks in Silvercreek. Still another was established at Blake, near River Styx. Despite these pioneering efforts, none grew into the huge conglomerate that ultimately became the Brickyard.

In 1904, William A. Ault, J.K. Durling (father of Dr. J.K. Durling, a Wadsworth physician in the 1930s and '40s), W.M. Wertz, Charles A. Curtis, E.S. Pardee and M.H. Leatherman purchased ten acres of land southwest of the village near the railroad tracks and began making bricks from what seemed to be an endless supply of good clay. With their $30,000 investment, they built six kilns and mass-produced bricks, reaching about six million annually at the onset.

The above mentioned men were not masons, industrialists or technicians; they were investors. William Ault not only invested in the brickyard but also

Located in Silvercreek, William Yockey was reputed to have had the first brick manufacturing establishment in Wadsworth. It did not remain there after the owners decided to farm the land instead.

J.K. Durling was responsible for many endeavors, including housing, industry and community leadership.

William Ault, former mayor of Wadsworth, an entrepreneur, racetrack owner and community catalyst.

in the horse racing track on College Street, west of Ault Street, a street named for him.

J.K. Durling invested in real estate as well as in the brickyard. Durling Drive is named after him, even though the venture he dreamed of never materialized beyond a couple houses still standing on Durling Drive. The first house on Durling Drive, a modified Dutch Colonial on the east side, was a Sears and Roebuck prefab that cost $1,200.

W.M. Wertz was a buggy maker and, according to the various legends about him, a moneymaker. He supplied capital for several ventures, some known and some not.

Charles Curtis was a banker who led the Wadsworth Savings and Trust. Watrusa Avenue is an acronym incorporating segments of the title. After leading the bank from 1919 until 1930, when the Depression claimed the bank as one of its hundreds of victims, the institution was reorganized under the name Citizens Bank. The Curtis statue placed in the cemetery is in memory of his young son, who died in an accident close to where the statue

The Curtis House, located opposite Woodlawn Cemetery. Their young son was killed near the home and buried across the street at the cemetery. A Curtis monument still stands in his memory.

is located. Upon his death, Curtis gave a considerable amount of money to Akron University (presently the University of Akron) for Curtis Cottage, now demolished.

E.S. Pardee was one of the dozens of Pardee offspring who came from money and invested in many enterprises throughout the village. His family members were among the first pillars of the community, producing judges, attorneys, physicians and high-ranking military officers. Pardee Street is named for his family.

Milton Leatherman invested not only in the brickyard but also in the newly formed telephone company that connected residents of Wadsworth with one another over copper wires. Leatherman Road is named for his family but not necessarily for Milton himself.

What started out as exploratory ventures on the Yockey Farm in Silvercreek finally ended up as the General Clay Products Company (GCPC), a Columbus firm that purchased the assets of the Wadsworth Brick and Tile Company in 1950. GCPC brought the manufacturing processes into the twentieth century under the leadership of Harold B. Epler, who had other brickyards in Columbus, Logan and Arthur, Ohio. Today, no trace of these efforts remains in Wadsworth, except for a retired executive from the firm, Patrick Brannigan, a number of former workers and at least one foreman, Bob Potts.

There are many stories about the brickyard. It was a clandestine (read, illegal) place for people to swim in the large reservoir formed where clay was excavated. It was the place where wreaths were placed for people who drowned in the pit. It was the place where some African American residents of Wadsworth lived while being employed as laborers in the kilns. It was the place where residents would go to pick up scraps of bricks for personal use—with or without permission. It was a popular place for couples to get lost in its vast acreage. It was the place that made Wadsworth known worldwide for the high-quality bricks created here and shipped abroad.

Fort Knox uses a specially constructed Wadsworth ceramic in the United States Mint, some of the Ford Motor Company buildings are made with Wadsworth bricks and structures in other countries carry the name and soul of Wadsworth bricks as monuments to our product.

Bricks continue to be made somewhere, but no longer in Wadsworth.

PART III

ART AND RECREATION

Musical Luminaries of Wadsworth

Wadsworth's early settlers were characterized as being dedicated only to hard work and endless toil, overcoming severe economic conditions, living with few or no luxuries and espousing only conservative values. This was probably true in the very beginning; however, as time went on (about seventy years of time, to be precise) life became a little more directed toward arts and recreation.

Of somewhat of a surprise for a community whose residents embraced stoic, disciplined and conservative values is the fact that one of the first artistic ensembles in the village was the Mandolin and Guitar Club, an organization whose instruments are usually associated with the romantic southern European nations rather than with the staid English and German pioneers who came to Wadsworth. Charter members of the Mandolin and Guitar Club were Horace Nice, director; Bessie Geib Bucher; Dave Geib; Gertrude Nicely Baker; Arthur Nice; Elsie Hard Osborn; Charles Yoder; Della Rickert Curry; Ida Rickert Warren; Frank Jordan; Ed Evans; Daisy Miller Garrison; Nettie Geib Schlabach; and Miss Hendershot.

More in keeping with the English/Germanic traditions were the many singing groups that existed throughout the village. Each of the churches had choirs and "singings" for church services. Additionally, there were choral

The Mandolin Band was the first musical ensemble organized in Wadsworth. Later, a band, an orchestra and several vocal ensembles were organized.

singing groups that were not associated with church services but were, nonetheless, attached to church congregations. The Normal, a conservatory of sorts, is where Emma Struggles Wuchter taught voice lessons to those who had natural talent. Brown's *Wadsworth Memorial* is replete with accounts of various singing groups composed of anyone who wanted to sing. Mrs. Wuchter would have none of that: auditions would determine whether the person had the voice for training or not.

EMMA STRUGGLES WUCHTER

Emma Struggles Wuchter was a highly respected music teacher in Wadsworth for many years in the late 1800s. Her marriage to Dr. George H. Wuchter, son of Jonas Wuchter of Republican embalming fame, gave her additional prominence. Her students became some of Wadsworth's most gifted piano and voice teachers and were regarded as possessing the same quality of artistry as Emma herself.

She was known as a hard taskmaster, one who demanded perfection. Those who were not willing to practice diligently or sacrifice beautiful days outside to sit indoors to go over the never-ending scales she assigned were not invited to continue under her tutelage.

Dr. George served in the Spanish-American War and was the only surgeon in the Eighth Ohio and Thirty-third Michigan Infantries. He suffered many infirmities as a result of microbes he acquired in Cuba during the war, and he had to cease practicing medicine when he came to Wadsworth because of health failure.

Dr. George had a beautiful white horse that was the pride of the family, as well as of the residents of the village. This horse carried him in the battlefield to aid wounded soldiers, and Dr. George became attached to him. After his return from war, he kept the horse in a barn that was located at the corner of Mill and Main Streets, where East of Chicago now stands. The horse was a "family member"; Emma loved him, revealing another side of the person whose reputation as a demanding teacher was a mantra.

It is not known whether Emma organized any of the vocal groups, but it is known that she was the resident authority in any group she joined. Equally, it was not known whether she aided Dr. George in the embalming profession after Jonas died, leaving Dr. George to continue embalming.

Emma and Dr. George's house was located directly across Main Street from Central School. It stood for many years until it was demolished in the late 1900s. The irony of the house was that it housed the embalming parlor in one portion and a music studio in another, almost a personification of the symbol for drama: a happy mask and a sad mask, side by side.

Divas of the Opera

Not Really

Wadsworth had an opera company. In truth, the company should have been called an *operetta* company, since its singers did not perform grand opera but operettas instead. Claude Hilliard, Lillian Rogers, George Fries, Bill Simester, Mollie McCarthy, Joe Bender, Luther Clubertson, Lester Dutt, Dave Straiton Jr. and George Witschey were involved. Clem Ebner was the design person.

Literary groups were formed throughout the village. What would now be called spelling bees were once called literaries and were popular not only among school students but adults as well. It should be noted that many of the adults had not had formal educations, and they were learning alongside their children. Literaries fostered a backdrop for not only spelling but also poetry, storytelling, acting, recitations, creative writing and reading clubs. Contests abounded between churches, families and even men and women. The literaries were not considered a competition per se but a forum for presenting entertainment to the villagers and instruction to the participants.

The Grand Army Band was organized in 1886 and featured three trombones, one tuba, four French horns, one English horn, one bass drum, three cornets and four clarinets. The uniform was, of course, blue, the color of the Union army. After the hype of the Civil War waned, the band was renamed the Cornet Band; however, the instrumentation did not change significantly, with the exception of there being more cornets in the latter

The Wadsworth Cornet Band was an outgrowth of an earlier band that grew slowly after the Civil War. Performances included a minimal repertoire of marches and spirited music.

band. Still later, it was called the City Band when it emerged as a larger unit with more and varied instruments after 1900.

The more dignified members of the community sought to have an orchestra, where serious music could be performed rather than just military-type marches. Some of the same members played in both the band and orchestra; nonetheless, there were fewer in the orchestra than in the band. The first orchestra featured only two violins, one bass viol, a tuba, one trombone, a flute and two cornets. Ira Rasor, Jonas Bowman, Dr. George H. Wuchter, Frank Coleman, Zeno Parmelee, O.L. Nolf, Frank Hunsberger and Wallace Brouse were in the first orchestra. Wallace Brouse also made violins and was known for fitting the violin to the size of the person (i.e., a small one for a child and a regular-sized one for adults). Later, his son, Avon, continued the art of violin making. It is of note that women did not perform in these ensembles.

Both band and orchestra regaled the community with music on a regular basis, the band always playing in the center of the village on Saturday nights and the orchestra on less frequent occasions, usually in homes or schools.

The first Wadsworth Orchestra developed when some band members wanted to play more serious music that was not of the march genre.

While the band was always in uniform when performing, the orchestra was always in formal black attire from head to toe, except for a white shirt. In reviewing the scant programs that are available, it is obvious that there was not a very comprehensive musical repertoire to be found in the performances. Most of the marches were Civil War marches and were played over and over again week after week, and the orchestral offerings were simplified classical selections, many times of religious origin.

Sports Stars and Racehorses

Those who were not musically inclined found their inner-self outlets through athletic events. Baseball, football and horse racing were the most popular sporting events. Until after 1900, basketball was rarely mentioned as a sport. Then, surprisingly, both men and women participated in basketball.

The first baseball field was at the corner of North Lyman and North Streets. It poorly resembled the sophisticated ball fields we have today. It did not have a diamond like today's fields; rather, the field was just that—a field with grass planted on it and a dirt path leading to the three bases and home plate. Today, there are many houses in that area. In the latter part of the 1800s, there were no houses, just open fields.

Wadsworth finally outgrew the first field and moved baseball a little to the south and a bit west, to what would be the east side of High Street, where the Huntington Bank and the stores toward the square are now located. At one time, this was a quarry where whetstone was extracted, but when a better vein was found east of the village, it was retired, leveled and made into a useable area that seemed fit for a ball field. There was also acreage east of what is now Trinity UCC, which was then the site of the Normal School. The ground was actually a recreation area for students at the Normal School (a playground of sorts) and ideally suited for "real" games. Because of this, games were played there, but not on Sunday, since playing games on Sunday was in violation of the village standards of conduct. (A strategy to get around this ruling will be discussed later.)

Going south on Lyman Street toward what is now Pine Street, looking east from Lyman to East Street, there was an open field that was not only vast but also had absolutely no obstructions, permitting heavy hitters to be comfortable with batting the ball as far as they wanted.

The first "official" basketball team consisted of high school girls in 1920. There were others before, but these were not organized as such.

It is interesting to note that in that area is a deep incline in the road, just east and south of Central Intermediate School between Broad and Pine Streets. This was usually flooded and impassable after heavy rain. As a result, there was a bridge from Lyman to Main for people to traverse. Although the bridge was not built to the standards of what would be acceptable today, it was actually called Bridge Street. It was vacated and torn down many years ago.

The field was nominally called Park Street Field and was the first to be fenced in, a requirement of inter-team "professional" competition. The Cleveland Spiders played an exhibition game at Park Street Field in 1895. The Spiders won, seven to five, but Wadsworth's Harry Mills hit a home run off baseball legend Cy Young.

Baseball was popular from its very beginnings. It began to become organized in Wadsworth in the late 1800s, with several teams that competed home and away.

The Silvercreek ball field served to allow games to be played on Sundays since an ordinance based on religion restricted such events in the village. People who supported the ordinance were offended that men used this field to circumvent the law.

Other baseball lots (some not distinguished enough to be called fields) were located on the west side of North Pardee Street, north of Prospect Street. One was called Lyle Field, named after the person who permitted the game to be played on his field. There are accounts that "permission" was never actually given; it was merely assumed. Another was on Bergey Street, and there was one on Bird Street. Bird Street still exists, but not in its original presentation or in the exact location where it was in the late 1800s.

Earlier, mention was made that games were not played in the village on Sundays. Only men or older boys played, and most of them worked six days a week and had only Sunday for practice and games. Silvercreek was outside the village limits; hence, the locals built a field south of the Erie Railroad tracks and west of the road that ran through Silvercreek (now called Silvercreek Road). They practiced there to circumvent the village ordinance that forbade anyone "over the age of fourteen years, to engage in sporting,

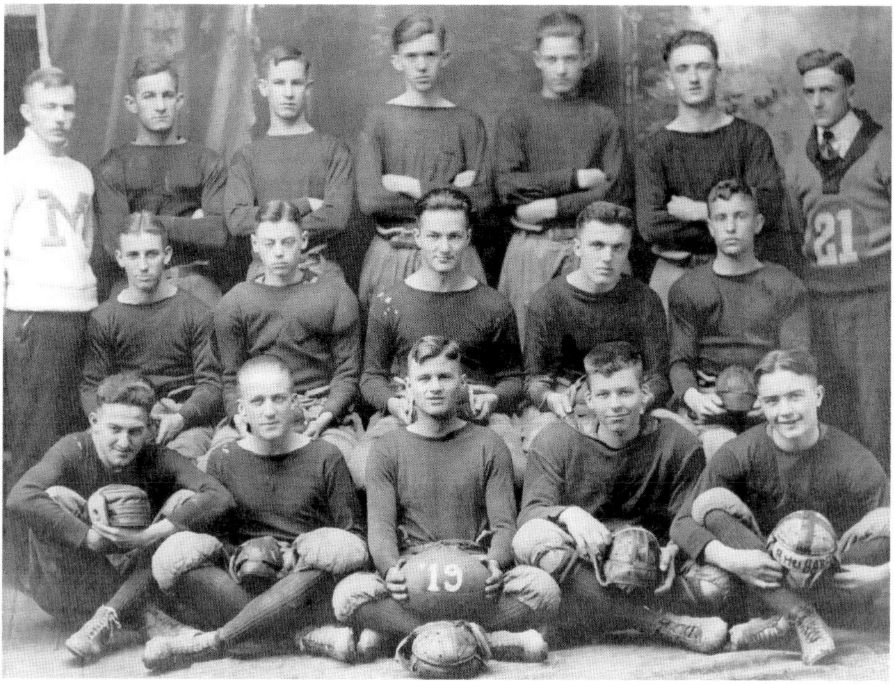

An early football team photographed in 1919. Wadsworth has always had a passion for football, but organized football was developed after some other sports had already been organized.

rioting, rowdying, or noisy or disorderly talk or conduct." Violators were fined up to forty dollars for this offense, a handsome sum for the time. Since the field was in Silvercreek, the team was known as the Silvercreek Ball Club and boasted some of Wadsworth's best ballplayers. The team had an area-wide reputation for winning. Some Wadsworth residents refused to participate in the Silvercreek practices because of the heavy feeling of guilt they felt for violating a village ordinance based on the religious commandment to keep the Sabbath holy.

Football, as we know it today, was once a far different game, both in popularity and in the manner in which it was played. In 1904, the Wadsworth football team played on Lyle Field (cited above) in uniforms consisting of knickers, black vests and long-sleeved shirts. Only the coach had the letter "W" on his shirt. Goal posts were not clearly marked, nor was the field lined. Players ranged from mid-teens to late teens and appear not to have worn protective pads or helmets.

ART WRIGHT

The "Wright" Man for the Job

Until the late 1920s, Wadsworth did not have much of a football legacy. Indeed, there were teams, there were games, there were stars and there were coaches, but the town still did not have much of a football legacy. Wadsworth did not have a field of any quality, teams did not have uniforms that did much more than cover the body for modesty and a bit of protection, there was no equipment except a football and games were played on Saturday afternoons since there were no lights for night games.

What Wadsworth did have was an energetic and willing group of boys and men who thirsted for the excitement of football. Had there been opportunities as we know them today, Wadsworth would have had multiple victories long before they became commonplace in the community. Conversations with men who were old in the late 1940s pointed to the frustration many of them had because there was not the support and organization that would have elevated their desires to reality.

In 1931, Art Wright came to Wadsworth. A husky and muscular man, he walked with the confidence of a person who had never suffered

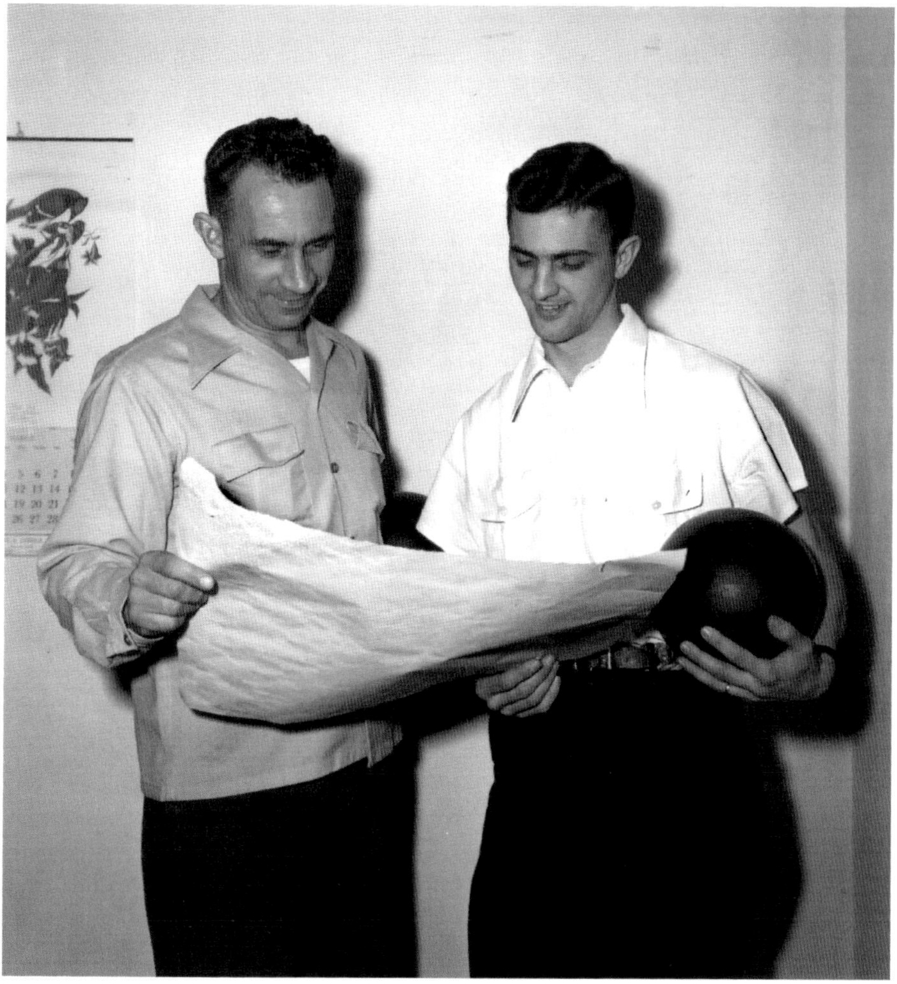

Art Wright is credited for developing the football program in Wadsworth and producing award-winning teams. Coach Russ Doan is on the right.

fear—certainly not induced by another person. He was strong, direct, opinionated and "wright." He had little patience for those who were not forthright, honest and sincere, and he respected those who were. He was apolitical. He did not care if he was "politically correct" or not; he cared only that he was "correct."

Art Wright was a tender father to those who needed tenderness, but after he dealt with a boy's tender spirits, he would build him into a strong, confident and productive man. His discipline was manifested through his stature, his voice, his directness and his reputation. He always stood erect, and when he wanted to command, he threw his head back ever so slightly, just enough so that the listener knew to accede to whatever he was saying. The furrow on his brow punctuated his message, signifying that discussion was neither needed nor requested. What was necessary had already been said.

Art came to Wadsworth to serve as coach but also had to teach. His academic discipline was social studies, and he was made a teacher of history to assist Willard Hunsberger with the increase in students Wadsworth High School experienced after Wadsworth became a city in 1931.

Born in Chicago in 1907, Art came to Barberton when he was nine years old. He went through the Barberton schools and played all sports in high school; rather, he *starred* in all sports in high school. He lettered in football, basketball, baseball and track—three times for each sport—and was captain of the football team in 1924. The basketball team on which he played won the coveted Northeastern Ohio Basketball Tournament title at Goodyear Gym the year he was captain. Unfortunately, it was later discovered that one of the players was overage, and Barberton had to forfeit the championship. Barberton residents believed for many years thereafter that, had they not had to forfeit the game, they would have been state champs.

Following graduation from Barberton High School, Art went to college at Riverside Military Academy at Gainesville, Georgia, where he was the quarterback of the team and won all-state recognition. He was all-Georgia in basketball as well, a real accomplishment for a "northerner." Art later enrolled in Mercer University in Macon, Georgia, where he led the team in scoring in 1926.

Art came back to Ohio, perhaps for his high school sweetheart, Elizabeth "Liz" Marvin, whom he married in Georgia. When he did come back, he began teaching at Wadsworth High School, where he stayed until he retired.

When Art came to Wadsworth, the Great Depression was two years old, an infant in its eleven-year scourge that caused deprivation, hunger and heartaches across an entire nation. Despite the odds, Art was able to grow the football program into a competitive force that was victorious over some of even the most formidable teams in surrounding communities.

Following the Great Depression, World War II broke out on December 7, 1941. Art, as almost every eligible man and some women in Wadsworth, was called to serve in the military. Art chose the navy and became a high-ranking officer and commander of a minesweeper. After serving for about four years, he was discharged from a naval base in California. He and some of his friends from communities near Wadsworth tried to get transportation home. None seemed to fit their schedules, so they hired a taxi, split the cost, and rode across the country to Wadsworth.

Art died of a sudden heart attack on July 5, 1965, at age fifty-eight, leaving a legacy that included teaching, coaching and, in later years, serving as principal. After his death, the Wadsworth Board of Education renamed Grandview Stadium to the Art Wright Stadium in his honor. He served under two superintendents—Frank Close and Maurice Burkholder—but he served thousands of students, of whom some owe their success to his being "wright."

Horse Racing

From Coal Yards to Racetracks

Horse racing was particularly popular in Wadsworth in the late 1800s—though today it is found only at racetracks—because there were so many horses, and nearly everyone was skilled at riding. Seth Baughman was known as the "Grand Old Horseman" in Wadsworth because he furnished horses for the Civil War, as well as those used to haul coal to customers from the mines in Silvercreek. Both of these ventures made him quite wealthy. Seth's forty-three acres were on the east–west road, now numbered 381 College Street. His daughter, Ida, married William Ault. What Seth did with his money after his death is not recorded; however, his son-in-law built a racetrack on what is now A-C Field. (A-C Field is named for the Athletic Club, despite stories connecting its name with Ault and College Streets, where it is located.)

Joining Ault in what was to become a destination in the village were F.M. Plank, Ira Everhard, Sam Cunningham, David Rickard, Sam Andrews and J.K. Durling. The original name for the racetrack was Wadsworth Driving Park Club. The track was a half mile in length and had a stand for the judges and sufficient room for spectators. The track was open for horse racing only during good weather. In winter, the inside of the track was flooded and used for ice-skating. Some residents remember skating on that rink in the 1930s and '40s. The horse racing track ceased operation when a severe flood washed out the lower end of the track. Efforts to reorganize and rebuild failed. The Wadsworth Athletic Club purchased it and made it into a ball field, therein retiring some of the smaller lots that had outgrown their usefulness.

Betting was part of the activity at the track, albeit in clandestine fashion. Upright Wadsworth citizens decried the practice, but it was hard to stop since the bets were not placed openly. There were reports of people coming from "bad places" to bet on horses. Some of the best sources regarding betting came from old-timers in Wadsworth who delighted in telling how much they made on betting. There are stories from some of the old-timers who worked at the Match in the mid-'40s and bragged about how much they won. Had they won what they said they won, they would not have been working at the Match!

Recreation for Women

As mentioned earlier, only men were permitted to engage in sports until after 1900, and even then, women were welcome in basketball only. They were not welcome in horse racing and certainly not in contact sports. Women had needs for creative and artistic expression and became agitated that they were being left out.

Taking the leadership role in organizing women was Mrs. C.A. Curtis, who invited thirteen women into her gaslit parlor on October 28, 1896, to form a cultural club, later to be named Followers of Pallas Athena (FPA), a reference to the Greek warrior goddess who has been a heroine of women for centuries. Village men quickly dubbed the organization "Forty Pretty Angels," an obvious attempt to denigrate the efforts of this cadre of courageous women who wanted to organize so they could express their many unheralded talents and strengths.

The original meeting in Mrs. Curtis's parlor resulted in other clubs for women to organize, including Sorosis (1907), the Art and History Class (1912) and Literature and Arts (1921)—all organizations founded to form social, artistic and intellectual alliances among women with common interests. They became powerhouses that coalesced the female fabric of the village. They still exist and are active today.

The Sorosis women at a formal dinner in 1925. Members took turns hosting the dinners.

In a written but unpublished history of Sorosis compiled by Janet Warner, a longtime member of Sorosis, Article IV of the bylaws states that the annual dues shall be one dollar. This continued for eighteen years, at which point they were established at two dollars by a vote of the entire body on March 23, 1925. It was not until sixty years later that they were raised to five dollars. Fee structures for the other two organizations were similar, giving rise to the understanding that their *raison d'être* was for social and general improvement for women and not any monetary orientation.

In later years, other organizations evolved for women, uniting those who entered the business and professional world. Because women were not involved in commerce until the twentieth century (and then progress was slow), they did not organize for several years after the first wave of women pioneered the movement.

For younger girls, the Campfire Girls formed in 1915 and began raising funds by selling refreshments at various athletic events. For boys,

Clyde Oplinger, one of Wadsworth's accomplished musicians and a bandleader, formed the Boy Scouts, an organization know nationwide but new to Wadsworth.

PRIZEFIGHTING

Prizefighting—usually without any prize for the winner—was a popular, nonscheduled sport in Wadsworth beginning in the 1850s on an informal "formal" basis. Coal miners, whose occupation commanded superior strength, gave men the confidence to take on anyone who was willing to fight. It was first thought that these fights resulted from those who had a "proclivity to the grape" and would fight after having had too much to drink; however, as the impromptu fights became more numerous, they were actually "staged" on Saturday nights in the center of the village. There was no formal billing for these fights, but the locals expected

Bar patrons in a South End bar poised to offer a friendly welcome to patrons they had not yet met.

The Cracker Barrel Crowd, a forerunner of present-day meet-for-coffee groups. The club was exclusive, requiring personal invitations and approval of the whole.

them and were never disappointed. Most of the bouts occurred on the east side of Main Street, where Domino's Pizza is located today. It is no coincidence that that is also where the saloon was located at the time.

There were also diversions for men not interested in any of the above activities, particularly the Cracker Barrel Crowd, which met in the alley behind what is now Domino's Pizza. These men did not participate in athletic events, did not joust or box, did not ride horses and did not meet to elevate their personal selves. They simply met, always at about lunchtime. There was a semblance of organization to this venture. Men only were invited to join the group, and only those invited could join. According to the 1895 roster, most of the men were merchants, professional people, industrialists or political figures. There is no evidence of the general public being invited to membership. Most of the conversations were about days gone by and discussions on the status of the world. The Cracker Barrel Crowd lasted for many years, probably evolving gradually into what are now the various groups of retirees who meet formally/informally each morning for coffee at various locations throughout the city.

There seemed to be something for everyone. It appeared there was a thirst for a higher order of life repressed during the first seventy years as the pioneers focused primarily on surviving. The human psyche thirsts for something beyond subsistence when necessities are satisfied. Wadsworth villagers found their satisfaction through arts and recreation.

PART IV

WADSWORTH AT HOME IN THE AIR

Early Wadsworth Housing Developments

Built and Housed Wadsworth's Legends

When present-day Wadsworthites think of housing developments, they think of Clearview Acres, Westgate, Highland Heights, Silver Knolls and others scattered throughout town. They also think the houses on Lyman, Highland, Humbolt, Fairlawn, Summit, Gordon, Overlook and Baird were always there since they have been there for so many years. In truth, the vast acreage in the northeast quadrant of the city, starting at the east end of the square, was once farmland.

The population of Wadsworth in 1890, before the industries started to build, was about fifteen hundred. Twenty years later, when the Injector, Match and Salt Companies were in their prime and expanding, it doubled in size to a little more than three thousand. By the time Wadsworth became a city in 1931, it had reached at least five thousand. All these people living here meant there was a need for more housing.

Shortly after Dr. Lyman died in 1905, his land, bounded on the west by what is now Lyman Street and extending north and east, was divided into individual lots for housing developments. This opened opportunities for expansion to the east. But why expand to the east rather than south, west

Dr. George Lyman, a physician, community leader, industrial developer and legacy in Wadsworth history.

or north? There is no question why the village did not expand to the south: that's where the factories and railroad tracks were. It resisted expanding to the west: that's where the cemetery was. Why not north? This area was farmland and was not available for development.

Another theory to explain the eastward expansion, in addition to the ones cited above, was that E.J. Young built his unique and stately home across from what is now Highland Avenue in 1923. With the Young Mansion as a drawing card, a portion of what is now Highland Avenue was constructed through the newly formed Lyman development. Realtors Schuyler and John Durling further subdivided Highland into salable lots and charged

The E.J. Young House, built on Broad Street in 1923, served as an anchor for other beautiful houses to be built in the area.

$500 each for them, a considerable amount at the time, but one that would attract only those who could build a distinguished house to reflect the developers' vision.

In 1912, John O. Licey, a River Styx native and attorney (as was his father) cut a swath through a portion of the Lyman property and named it Humbolt Avenue, after an agnostic scientist. John did not uphold the scientist's agnosticism, but he was impressed with the man's science. There were comments about the poetic justice that transpired later in that there is a parochial school at one end of the street and a large church at the other.

Humbolt didn't go anywhere except into a wooded area. To make it a viable street, Licey cut Boyer Street from where it ended somewhere in the Lyman-to-Highland area and connected it to Humbolt Street. At the same time, the German Reformed Church (now the United Church of Christ) was in the process of building its new place of worship, so Licey purchased the old wooden church, took it apart board by board, rebuilt it at the corner of Humbolt and Boyer (on the northwest corner of the road going through Durling Park) and made it into Wadsworth's first apartment building. There were five apartments, each consisting of five rooms with closets. Many older residents knew this house as the Pumpkin because it was big, square and painted orange.

John Licey was drafted into military service for the Spanish-American War and served his entire time as a private. One of the fortunate ones to return home after the war, he sought to find something that would enhance his standard of living from recently discharged soldier and country attorney to prosperous citizen. He saw the future was going to be growth in Wadsworth, and he wanted to be part of it.

As he looked at the Lyman Farm (bordered by Lyman and Broad Streets) and recognized that people would want to build in that section of town since some nice houses were already there, he took a giant leap and started his own development venture. He was competing against men of means, such as the Durlings. As will be addressed later, the Spring Hill development that was the Schuyler/John Durling child failed. Licey reasoned that one reason it failed was that it was too far away—Durling Drive is about a mile from the center of town—from where the nicer homes were already established. His logic prevailed. The Humbolt development prospered, with about fifty houses being built there before the street was completely filled. John Licey became known for building quality, unpretentious houses at a reasonable cost in a location adjacent to some of the extraordinary houses only a few hundred feet west.

John O. Licey (his middle name was Othello) was a learned man who was highly versed in Shakespeare and had many friends of means, both in Wadsworth and in surrounding communities. On one occasion, after Thanksgiving, he went to a dinner at a friend's home in Akron and complained of feeling ill. The friend, wanting to be hospitable, invited John O. to eat more. The more he ate, the worse he felt. After arriving home, he died, much to the astonishment of his friends and family. John's father never got over the grief he felt at having lost his son and law partner. John O. was buried in the mausoleum at Woodlawn Cemetery, but the crypt was not sealed immediately so his father could see him again. Finally, his father, Alvin, realized John O. would never come back, so he ordered the crypt sealed. He asked his good friend Joe Bender to accompany him to the crypt for the final sealing. In remembrance of his deceased son, Alvin took a cane carved with Indian figures that John O. had purchased in Mexico and carried it constantly until his death. Upon his death, he willed the cane to Joe Bender; it became an item of the Bender estate when Joe died.

Schuyler built his own house, on the corner of Highland and Highland Place. Leslie Hartzell built on the other corner toward Broad Street. Ohio Match superintendent Elmer Swartz built a huge brick house on the north side of Broad (demolished to make room for the addition to Sacred Heart School), across from the Young House. Wayne Young built on the southeast corner of East Street and Broad, just east of his father's house on the other corner (now the Methodist church parking lot). Other Ohio Company executives, such as Charles Allen, chief engineer of the Ohio Injector Company; Don Williams, a Match executive; and Charles Warner, from the Ohio Salt, also built on Highland Avenue. Lawrence Fiely, from the Ohio Salt, built on Woodland, across the street and a little north of Ervin Young, a vice-president of the Injector, whose house stood as an icon on the street. Don Young built on the north side of Broad Street at the top of the hill. Sitting back from the road about two hundred feet, the house looks like a smaller version of an English castle.

It was not long until Highland Avenue became *the* street on which to live, so much so that the street was paved with brick. Many of the other streets in town were not paved, especially not with brick.

Farther east, realtors Schuyler and John Durling developed Spring Hill, a name no longer associated with the failed development that includes Durling Drive. Following this failure, the brothers developed the area north of Broad Street, but still on the hill, as Colonial Heights, yet another name no longer associated with houses on Baird, Gordon and Overlook Avenues.

Heirs of the J.K. Durling family gave what is now a good portion of Durling Park. According to some older Wadsworth residents—most of them deceased by now—Durling Park was placed where it is to accent the prestigious houses built around it to the north and south. Others believe the land was donated because the elevation, terrain and drainage problems made it unsuitable for building. The elevation of Humbolt as compared with Woodland is dramatic.

The original parcel that comprised the park was increased when Joe Bender donated some of his land to build a road though the park to connect Humbolt to Prospect, opening an entrance to Crestwood and to Woodland by turning left on Prospect. The road through Durling Park was vacated several years ago as a safety measure to the highly utilized park. Also, John Licey donated the land on which he rebuilt the church building (or as indicated earlier, the Pumpkin).

After the road was cut through Durling Park to Prospect, the Crawford Real Estate Company began developing Crestwood Avenue north of Prospect. This was also part of the original Lyman Farm. At that time, Crestwood and Highland did not have a paved surface to go to Route 261.

James K. Durling, father of Dr. James K. Durling, had a stellar beginning in Wadsworth in that he was instrumental in founding the first bank in Wadsworth in 1873 and was mayor from 1892 to 1894. Highly recognized for his financial acumen and success as a civic leader, he was selected by Marvin Kent, who started the railroad that eventually came through Wadsworth, to plow the first furrow for the extension of the Atlantic and Great Western Railroad west of Kent. Kent—or, as it was known then, Franklin Mills—is about thirty miles from Wadsworth. For a Wadsworth resident to be selected for such an auspicious event suggests Durling merited a strong measure of respect beyond Wadsworth, respect well deserved because of the character he portrayed.

After Durling succeeded in all his other business ventures, he decided to continue with others who were involved with the newest big moneymaker: development. He chose a portion of what had been the Falk Farm years earlier for his venue. Again, he either chose the wrong location or his marketing strategy was ineffective because the attempt was a failure. This did not deter him from continuing with his interest in Wadsworth's growth or dampen his zeal to make substantial contributions to the community through his talents and treasures.

Raymond Holcomb Sr., father of Ray Holcomb, former principal in the Wadsworth Schools and still living as of this writing, built some of the houses on Humbolt and most of the ones on Crestwood Avenue. Before Crestwood was opened for a housing development, it was a vast acreage used for farming. These houses still stand as testimonies to the quality of workmanship that went into the "new" homes in the early twentieth century. Hardwoods were plentiful around Wadsworth in earlier times, and as a result, the houses were fitted with hardwood flooring, trim and cabinetry. In many houses, even the framing was hardwood.

Bill Caine built an expansive house east of Crestwood Avenue on seven acres of land in 1937. Bill's house was considered the last of the Ohio Company executives' large and symbolic houses. Talk around town centered on what was a novelty at the time: an automatic garage door opener. It did not work by activating radio waves, as is the case today, but according to those who knew, it worked by the driver pressing a button that would engage an electromagnet in the car that communicated with another magnet in the ground. The ground magnet would then activate the mechanism that opened the door.

Although focus was given to the east side of Wadsworth because of the grandiose homes being built there, the area north of town was also enjoying a steady but quieter growth spurt.

Ross Trump, of the Excel Rubber Company (south of the far end of First Street and almost to the railroad tracks), built the brick Colonial house on the west side of High Street. After his sudden and untimely death, Carl Shaffer purchased the house and maintained it in pristine condition. The house has passed through several hands since the Shaffers owned it; nonetheless, it still reflects its dignified aura.

Tolbert Simcox lived in the big brick house on the west side of High Street on his farm that extended from High to West Streets and from North Street to about where Route 261 dead-ends into High Street. Tolbert died in 1910, and his farm was sold to the Myers and Crawford real estate dealers. They subdivided the farm and cut two streets through it, naming them after Tolbert Simcox. For years, people thought the street was named after a Mr. Tolbert and a Mr. Simcox; yet neither of those two street names was associated closely with anyone in Wadsworth, despite the presence of Simcox families in Wadsworth. Research showed that the realtors thought the two names sounded like surnames and attached them to the two streets.

Just north of the Simcox Farm was the Franks Farm; however, Franks had sold the farm to Loren Way earlier. Sometime in the beginning of the 1920s, Way realized he did not want to farm the 117 acres and sold them to William Good and Henry Wolf, two names easily identified in Wadsworth. It follows, then, that Wolf and Good Avenues were named for them. Franks Avenue was named for the original owner.

Today, there are numerous housing developments that future historians will report were not there in the latter part of the twentieth century. From wilderness, to settlement, to village to city, Wadsworth builds as Wadsworth grows.

CURRY, BALDWIN AND BRENNEMAN

Their Air Designs Finally Took Off!

Most Wadsworth residents think that the airport mentality started in the mid-1950s, when a few people got together to level, drain and prepare the ground in southwest Wadsworth. While this is the effort that produced the present airport, there were several other attempts in earlier years to put air travel at Wadsworth's doorstep, all of which failed.

Not too many years after the Wright brothers flew their first airplane successfully and later made improvements on it, exhibition teams flew around the state to promote this new venture: air travel. Almost no one in Wadsworth had ever seen an airplane, so when one came over, crowds of people would go outdoors to catch a glimpse of what appeared to be a wing with a motor on it and a person sitting in the middle of the wing. The plane's altitude was never too high, but in some cases, some early planes would be able to soar several thousand feet above the ground.

While most people were exhilarated by something flying through the air besides birds, some were not. Reports from old-timers cite that many farmers were horribly upset because cows, horses and other livestock would be pasturing in fields and would become so frightened at the roar of the plane's engine that they would stampede. Animals had become accustomed to the trains going by, but the sound the steam engines was nothing compared with the explosive sounds of the internal combustion engine of the plane.

Needless to say, the enterprising barnstormers did not electrify people with much interest in air travel. Most thought it to be a flash-in-the-pan type of enterprise—just as the automobile had been a few years earlier—and certainly not an idea that would ever take off (no pun intended).

Nonetheless, the few planes that passed over Wadsworth did catch the fancy of some of the residents, and in July 1929, some fifteen years after the beginning of the flights mentioned above, E.S. Curry introduced his good friend B.F. (Shorty) Fulton at the Rotary Club meeting. Shorty Fulton was a legend in the Akron area; the municipal airport in Akron was even named after him.

Shorty's presentation was followed by that of pilot C. Shirley, who continued to tout the advantages of an airport for every community to bolster economic development. To give emphasis to this concept, funeral

Glen Brenneman, a pharmacist, astute businessman, generous philanthropist and community leader, was regarded as a legend in Wadsworth.

director J.B. Hilliard, a guest at the Rotary Club from the Lions Club, read a letter from Standard Oil of Ohio offering its plane to Wadsworth any time the city needed it *IF* there were an airport here. Standard Oil had just purchased a plane that was used to transport its officials but also to give air transportation a boost in a world that had not yet accepted it as a viable travel alternative. It has been suggested that John D. Rockefeller, the founder of Standard Oil who married Wadsworth's Laura Spelman, still maintained a faint association with Wadsworth—hence, the offer.

The Rotary and Lions Clubs collaborated in this endeavor and appointed E.S. Curry, Dr. H.A. Baldwin and Glen Brenneman—all Rotarians—to a committee to explore the possibility of Wadsworth's building an airport.

E.S. Curry even arranged for the Goodyear dirigibles, later called blimps, to come to Wadsworth to give more impact to the airport initiative.

The date of the meeting—July 1929—preceded Black Friday, the big financial crash of October 29, 1929, by only three months. Many believed that had the crash not occurred, the dream of Wadsworth's having an airport as early as 1930 would have become a reality since three powerhouse personalities were behind it and two very active service clubs espoused it. As it was, the Great Depression, eleven years long, delayed many innovative ideas from materializing. This said, the hope in the minds and hearts of air travel enthusiasts did not wane. In fact, one of Wadsworth's own, Sam Griesmer, became a pilot for Eastern Airlines and was regarded as an air-transport hero among other Wadsworth enthusiasts. Sam actually landed a plane in Wadsworth in the early '30s. Throngs of people went to the site to see the plane, still a novelty to many. Planes flying overhead looked like toys; seeing the size of one up close was rare.

Air travel was so rare that if anyone did fly, he or she would make the newspapers. In the summer of 1929, Captola Breyley Forker, daughter of Mr. and Mrs. A.W. Breyley of 253 Broad Street, flew from California to Wadsworth as a guest of Marvel Crosson, female altitude ace. The twenty-eight-hundred-mile trip took twenty-eight hours of flying time, with stops in Phoenix and Tucson, Arizona; Lordsburg, New Mexico; El Paso and Fort Worth, Texas; Tulsa, Oklahoma; Kansas City, Kansas; St. Louis, Missouri; Indianapolis, Indiana; Columbus and Cleveland, Ohio; and, finally, to Wadsworth by car.

The reason for the trip was to promote air travel and to help organize the Aviation Country Club, a venture to bring together people who were interested in air travel. They picked Wadsworth as a terminal point because of Captola, but the trip coincided with the formation of the committee to bring an airport to Wadsworth as early as 1930.

Although the initial impetus for building an airport and developing air travel was stonewalled by an economic catastrophe in 1929, the germ never died. In 1954, Dr. N.J.M. Klotz, Dan Weltzein, Joe Klosterman, Wayne Forrer, Richard Kimmel, Wade Russell Riggs, Robert Fahl, John Puglisi, Robert Ahl, William Forrer, Stanley MacMichael, C. McDowell and Frank Randall energized their love for flying by developing what is now the Wadsworth Municipal Airport. Land was leased to this venture for a five-year period with options to continue operation if the airport succeeded. The airport is still extant and continues to grow.

The Wadsworth Airport

Not "Grounded" by Stormy Opposition

In the early 1950s, Dr. Nevin J.M. Klotz, a respected and popular Wadsworth physician, was one of many volunteers who boarded a bulldozer and began carving out a nearly mile-long strip of farmland, owned by the city in southwest Wadsworth, to make a runway for an airport that was already completed in the imaginations of several Wadsworth air enthusiasts. At one point, the bulldozer malfunctioned on a Sunday afternoon. Dr. Klotz and Dan Weltzein, whose passion for flying will be discussed later in this section, called garage owner Henry Carrino to repair the bulldozer engine. He did so. After the repair, without fanfare, fury or ceremony, Dr. Klotz hopped on the bulldozer once again and began smoothing out the ground that was to give support to the dreams of the many people who pioneered the realization of personal air travel in Wadsworth.

A modern airplane that is commonplace at the two airports in Wadsworth.

After more than eighty years of dreaming, Wadsworth now has two airstrips and a promise from the Federal Aviation Administration to expand the present airport, but not without roadblocks along the way. Many attempts have been made to close the airport, citing noise and danger, expense of operations, the withdrawal of the Airmen's Association as airport operators and resistance to extending the runway for fear jets would be able to land, therein causing even more noise. These and many more reasons abound with no ready answers. Yet the momentum for having an airport in Wadsworth begun in the early part of the twentieth century continues.

Adversity never "grounds" passion.

FROM MODEL PLANES TO "PLANE" LIVING

The thought of bringing airplane enthusiasts together as suggested by Captola Forker did not escape later visionaries. Dan Weltzein conceived the idea of establishing a development that would include an airstrip, a hangar, homes with a "garage/hangar" that could accommodate small planes and a community that would give air travel legitimacy and meaning.

Dan is the son of Clyde and Geneva Everhard Weltzein; he was born in 1931 in Wadsworth. Geneva became an airplane enthusiast, partly because she lived with Dan and partly because she felt the thrill of flying. She never learned to drive an automobile, but she could fly a plane. She also wrote a column for the Wadsworth *News-Banner* entitled "What's Going On Up There."

Dan became fascinated with flying as a child. As a boy, he had a real but stationary airplane in his back yard that he fired up from time to time to the hair-raising fright of neighbors, who thought a plane was crashing into their homes.

Dan was a fearless, adventurous, risk-taking and, above all, free- and forward-thinking visionary. His passions included anything fast or nontraditional. He was a motorcycle enthusiast; he rode at high speeds and had twenty-one almost-fatal accidents. With humor as his medicine, he told about sliding across a busy street in Wadsworth on his way to school one morning, hitting a car, flying over the hood and landing on the lawn facedown. He quipped, *"I was a little late for school that morning."* On another occasion, he and one of his riding friends were coming from west of Wadsworth, and since they had not tried riding the bike while lying on their stomachs with their legs extended over the back of the motorcycle, they thought they would try it. This unconventional posture for riding was predictably not the best idea, adding yet another accident to the list of almost-fatal crashes Dan endured.

Dan's father owned a repair garage and could have underwritten the costs of airplanes, motorcycles, insurance, attendant expenditures, etc., but being a good father, he placed the responsibility for payment on Dan. When Dan presented his vision to the president of the bank about building Skypark, the officers there were excited, giving Dan the encouragement to continue with what has become one of Wadsworth's unique features.

Post Office

Once a "Male" Thing

As primitive as it was, in early Wadsworth, letters and packages were delivered to the settlement from distant places, a service that was brought to the New World from European countries, especially England, the place of origin of many of Wadsworth's first settlers.

In the very beginning, Wadsworth's almost nonexistent population had to wait for weeks for mail from family and relatives living in Connecticut, where family and friends resided. The route was most circuitous. It went from Connecticut to New York to Philadelphia, then across the wide expanses of Pennsylvania and finally to Ohio. When it reached Ohio, it took several more days because this settlement was located on the very western edge of the Connecticut Western Reserve.

Mail was delivered by horse and rider. There was not a systematized postal service as we understand it today. Individual people were contracted to take mail from one place to another, many times simply because that person might be going in that direction.

In 1823, Abel Dickinson was appointed the first postmaster of the village. This merely meant he was recognized as being the person who would accept any mail coming to the village and would be responsible for expediting or releasing mail to the rightful addressee. He was also responsible for finding someone to take the mail to the nearest pickup point, sometimes miles away.

Dickinson remained the responsible person for forty-three years, always operating the post office from his home.

In 1866, when the village was incorporated, it built a small frame building on Aaron Pardee's property, close to what would now be the intersection of Watrusa and College Streets. After the town hall was built in 1867, the post office was moved there. At this time, Henry C. Pardee became responsible for the mail.

The mail service remained in the town hall for more than forty-five years. The quarters became cramped, and the town hall was crumbling, so the postmaster decided to move the postal service from that location to a storefront in the Rickard Block on the east side of Main Street, almost where the American Legion is now located. This was done in 1907 under the leadership of then postmaster Morgan Neath, an appointee of President Theodore Roosevelt.

At about this time, Wadsworth began organizing a postal service that was somewhat reflective of the embryonic system emerging at the federal level. There was no mail delivery in the early days. People would come to the center of the village to claim any mail they might have. Even as late as the mid-1880s, Don Albert Pardee would ride a horse from his "mansion" on Stony Ridge Road (now Reimer Road) to the center of town to pick up his mail.

Despite the village being in compliance with the format of the federal postal service, Wadsworth had not yet achieved a strong enough status to merit any financial assistance from the government to operate an official post office. The federal postal service required a certain volume of mail to be dispatched through a community before declaring it worthy of government recognition. Postmaster Neath, as all those responsible for the mail in previous years, had to pay rent for the quarters, purchase and maintain his own postal equipment (wagons, horses, sorting boxes, stamps, etc.) and had to pay personnel who might assist him with the mail. According to some early records, he was paid little for his work, leaving him only a small pittance to live on.

After some growth in the village and more activity in the post office, the federal government raised the status of the Wadsworth unit to third class, therein qualifying it to have the government pay for what Morgan Neath had to underwrite earlier.

It was not until September 1, 1913, that, through careful budgeting, Postmaster Neath was able to employ the first mail carriers: Lloyd Kreider and Benjamin Neff. Mr. Kreider carried mail to the entire north side of the village, and Mr. Neff, the south. To put this in perspective, the village extended only to about North Street to the north and to a couple streets south of the railroad to the south—all sparsely populated. The eastern limits were about fifteen hundred feet to the east of the center of the village and even less to the west. There were occasional houses beyond these boundaries, sparsely situated in all directions. It is not known whether the carriers served houses outside these boundaries. In the event that one or the other of the two mail carriers was not able to function on a particular day, Walter Smith was pressed into action as a substitute.

The quarters in the Rickard Block became cramped as a result of more people moving into Wadsworth. William Wells built a fairly large building at the south end of the business block on the west side of Main Street in the early 1920s, then known as the Wells Building and now known as 150 Main Street. The footage was ideal for a larger post office, so it was moved there and remained there until 1937, when the new post office was built on Broad Street.

Early airmail service lacked sophistication and was expensive and irregular.

Before moving into the Wells building, the postal service moved a huge United States Postal Service safe into that location. In 1937, when the new post office was built, the safe was to have been moved, but the logistics were so overwhelming that the government decided to donate the safe to the new occupants of the building, the Ackerman and Kahn families, who owned and operated the B&B Cut-Rate Store, which moved from its location at the corner of Mill and Mains Streets (now East of Chicago) to the Wells Building.

WORTH WESTENBARGER

Worth Westenbarger was postmaster when the operation was moved to the Wells Building. Although there are still surviving descendants of some of the earlier postmasters (daughter of Willard Thomas, son of William Dague, children of Barras Birkbeck, children of Bill Gross), Worth's children would be the oldest still living. An interview with Glen Westenbarger, the older of his two sons (Don is the other one), provided firsthand information about the postal service in Wadsworth eighty years ago. Additionally, an unpublished account of the family history gave additional information.

According to an unpublished document entitled "Zachary Taylor Westenbarger," Worth was born on November 17, 1896, and married the former Alma Beck in 1922. Alma's only sister, pharmacist Clara, married pharmacist and pharmacy owner Glen Brenneman. Stories about Beck Street being named for the family are unfounded.

Worth was the son of Benjamin Westenbarger, a North Carolina native and Lutheran minister who served as pastor of the Acme Lutheran Church (now known as Jerusalem Lutheran Church) on Acme Hill. He also served the Loyal Oak Lutheran Church during his tenure in Wadsworth. Benjamin's ministry brought Worth to Wadsworth, where he stayed and became a productive contributor to the community through his many activities, postmaster among them.

In the 1930s, when the country was mired in the Great Depression, everything was slow, including postal service. Stamps were sold in denominations from a half cent up to ten cents, with few people ever buying the latter. Postcards were popular since they were the least expensive. For this reason, there are hoards of postcards from that era that are collectors' items today.

One of the historic events that occurred during Worth's postmaster years was the bicentennial of George Washington's birth of February 22, 1732. Stamps commemorating the date were in abundance, and despite the necessity to conserve in any way possible during the difficult times, Worth purchased a sheet of commemorative stamps, which he passed on to Glen and which Glen has kept for nearly eighty years.

Worth was a young father during his postmaster years but was able to keep in close touch with kindergartner Glen since the school was across the street from the post office. Worth would wait for Glen at lunchtime, walk him to their home at 308 Lyman Street, eat lunch and then walk Glen back to finish the school day. Worth had no car at that time, something very common during the Depression.

The post office was next to another historic building mentioned in *Remembering Wadsworth: From Pioneers to Streetcars*. The Wuchter House was the one used by Jonas Wuchter to embalm Republicans while Ephriam Kremer embalmed Democrats north of the center. That house remained there until recent years with limited occupancy.

The site of the post office annex (as it in now known after the new post office was built on Lyman Street) was the home of the Reverend Samuel B. Leiter, pastor of the Reformed Church, now the United Church of Christ. The government purchased the home from Reverend Leiter's heirs and broke ground in 1936. The completed building was dedicated on May 22, 1937, with Mayor H.J. Hall presiding and Congressman Dow W. Harter delivering the address.

The Broad Street facility was the first United States government building erected in Medina County. This was of some significance; hence, on August 5, 1937, all of Broad Street east of Lyman Street was closed to traffic for another dedication, this time with then postmaster William I. Dague presiding and postmaster general James A. Farley, a Franklin D. Roosevelt appointee, giving the address.

It is of some degree of coincidence that Theodore Roosevelt elevated the post office in Wadsworth to a third-class designation, therein making Wadsworth finally eligible for federal funding, and Franklin D. Roosevelt appointed the postmaster who dedicated the first federal building in Medina County. Two postal benchmarks were recognized by two different Roosevelts.

Another fact of national significance is that the United States Treasury Department commissioned artist F. Thorton Martin, of Glenville,

W.I. Dague, the postmaster when the new post office was built in 1937. President Franklin Roosevelt sent the postmaster to dedicate the building since it was the first federal building in Medina County.

Artist drawing of early settlers arriving in Wadsworth.

Connecticut (close to where many Wadsworth people originated), to paint a large oil painting entitled *They Came as Wadsworth's First Settlers.* This painting hung in the post office until the new facility on Lyman Street was built. The painting is now displayed in the council chambers of Wadsworth City Hall. There are many accounts of this masterpiece having been commissioned by the WPA; it was not, according to some references. But according to *Soul of a People*, a documentary on the Great Depression, the painting was, indeed, underwritten by the Works Progress Administration (WPA). There is no documentation to support either claim, except for conflicting notations made by each entity.

Although he is now somewhat forgotten as a painter, F. Thorton Martin was a highly respected painter of the time and served for many years as an art adviser for the motion picture industry in Hollywood.

In *Remembering Wadsworth: From Pioneers to Streetcars*, mention is made that the post office in Wadsworth was overloaded with a half-million copies of the *Young Folks' Gem*, a newspaper written by George Bennett. While this is, indeed, factual, the volume of mail did not continue after Bennett's early death (at age twenty-one or twenty-three, depending on whose testimony one accepts) and the demise of the paper sometime later. Had it continued, the Wadsworth Post Office would have been elevated to a higher class many years earlier.

Postmasters who served Wadsworth after the turn of the century and for the next fifty years were: William J. Swisher, 1903; Morgan Neath, 1907; William A. Ault, 1915; Frank B. Malaney, 1922; Harry Liebhart, 1924; Worth D. Westenbarger, 1928; Willard D. Thomas, 1933; William I. Dague, 1934; and Barras G. Birkbeck, 1954.

Postmasters are usually appointees of the political party of the president of the United States. It is for this reason that there are frequent changes in local postmaster positions. From the time the postal service became systematized, the price of postage has ranged from one-half cent (for a postcard) to the present forty-two cents for a first-class letter.

PART V

WADSWORTH'S COLORFUL CHARACTERS

Big Andy

A Sizeable Legend

Wadsworth was a magnet for eastern and southern European immigrants who came to work in the Match Shop. Among these immigrants were fifty Italian families, a good number from the Slavic nations and the rest from individual eastern European nations. Germans, who gravitated mainly to manufacturing jobs and farming, constituted the largest contingent, making up about 20 percent of the population.

One of those who came from the vast regions of Russia was Big Andy. Big Andy was about six feet, nine inches tall and had a ruddy, almost giantlike physique. He did not have a wife with him—at least not that anyone was aware—and he lived on First Stret in a house he built himself. His mode of livelihood was simple. He went from store to store and collected cardboard boxes, cutting them up and selling them when he had accumulated a good supply. Earlier, he had worked at the Match, but he did not stay too long for reasons known only to Big Andy.

He had a loud, deep, stereotypical Russian voice that was frightening to small children and some adults. His size made the timbre of his voice even more overpowering, but inside his giant body was a warm and loving being.

Big Andy walked the streets of Wadsworth for more than thirty years, leaving an unforgettable mixture of charm and curiosity as his legacy.

He was a legend in the downtown area during the 1910s, '20s, '30s and early '40s, but he also traveled away from downtown, always walking since he did not have any other means of transportation. He carried his cardboard boxes in a rustic wooden cart that was affixed to two iron wheelbarrow wheels.

Big Andy had a last name, but people never used it, even if they knew it. The closest we can come to a last name is Kalidinsky (also spelled Klidnsky). This could be a transliterated spelling, since his name would have been written in the Cyrillic alphabet, the alphabet Russians use.

Big Andy was born in 1879 in Minsk, Russia, in present-day Belarus, separated from the Baltic Sea by Estonia, and came to Wadsworth in 1913, two years after he arrived in America. He spoke English, albeit with a heavy accent and broken structure; nonetheless, he made himself understood. Questions posed to him about his origins were met with a hearty and evasive brushoff, akin to a lion clearing his throat. There are those in town who believed he left a wife in Russia. Big Andy would neither verify nor deny this, but he did admit to having come from an unusually large family. He was equally as evasive about whether he had children.

Big Andy told of several brothers, two of whom were guards at the Kremlin. Both of these brothers were taller than Andy—an estimated seven feet tall, as demonstrated by Big Andy putting his hand edgewise on top of his head to show their heights.

Big Andy's rugged features, heavy mustache and unshaven beard made him look older than his years, but he was only sixty-nine when he died on July 11, 1948. He is buried in section 12, lot 29, south grave 1, according to Woodlawn Cemetery superintendent Denny Kreider. Reverend Mathes, then pastor of Trinity United Church of Christ, conducted the service. According to cemetery records, the person responsible for burying Big Andy was Tommy Lucas, then mayor of Wadsworth. This would imply that it was an indigent burial, since the city is mandated by law to bury those for whom relatives cannot be located. To the best of anyone's knowledge, there were no family members who could be found or who were present at his funeral. Despite his frugal existence, he has a dignified and stately monument above his grave. Whether he arranged for this before his death or whether someone else provided it for him is a question to which there is no ready answer because of privacy laws.

Big Andy liked dandelions and picked them in the outlying fields. After picking a goodly supply, he carried them home in a sack. There are stories about parents' using Big Andy's natural frightening qualities to control their children by telling them that he carried kids who didn't behave in the sack. There are still people in Wadsworth who are approaching their eighties who remember the threat.

Big Andy was extremely friendly, especially toward ladies. In the days he roamed Wadsworth streets, older ladies would try to avoid him because he would approach them with conversation, probably engendered by loneliness but interpreted by the ladies as social aggression. He always wore the same clothes, but he never looked as if he were not clean—only disheveled. His greeting was always loud and spontaneous; he never waited to be greeted first. His "hello" was more of a "hal-oo!" He never seemed to be angry, only lonely. People who stopped to talk with him were regaled with Russian lore. One of his favorite tales was about running after wild boars and feeling lucky to grab even a hunk of their hair. He told about his brothers wrestling one another and other village boys. When questioned about relative size and its impact on the outcome of the wrestling match, he said that all the boys in the village were "beeg, strrrong." When he laughed, everyone on both sides of the street could hear him. Big Andy never did "soft."

When Big Andy walked into stores asking if there were any empty boxes, he would stand in the doorway and bellow his question in a volume that resonated throughout the store, almost causing the walls to tremble. People who were not accustomed to his thunderous outbursts would freeze in fright. Storekeepers knew him and, if they saw him first, would forestall his query with the appropriate answer before his question could be asked. If the owner indicated that there were no boxes, Big Andy would turn around and leave the store without comment. If he learned there were some, he would go to where the boxes were stored and cut them up on the spot. When he pulled out his knife to do this, he did it with such theatric flair that the act itself was frightening. His knife was long with a white ivory handle that was worn and seasoned-looking. The blade did not seem to fold into the handle of the knife; instead, he kept it in a sheath attached to his belt. The ease with which he could slice up boxes with one swipe was testament to how sharp the blade was. When asked how he kept his blade so sharp, he said, "Wit a shtrop"—probably a length of leather. Big Andy used the same knife as an eating utensil, whether as a fork, spoon or knife, depending on what the cuisine required.

Big Andy died. We know when and where. We know where he is buried and who buried him. We know that he has a beautiful stone over his grave. We don't know anything about his last days, but we do know that he will now be chronicled among the legendary personalities who gave Wadsworth a tangy flavor that served to spice up its otherwise unexciting existence for a good forty years.

ROY MOORE

Skated into the Hearts of Wadsworth

Roy was a champion roller-skater, or so he said. His Santa tummy, short legs and five-foot-seven frame belied this claim. In his younger days, Roy skated all over town on his steel-wheel roller skates.

Roy Moore's headquarters. He stored materials for his many occupations in this building. It is not known whether he lived here.

Seeing was believing. He *was* an excellent skater and seemed to know every bump in every sidewalk. To the best of anyone's knowledge, he never fell and was never hit by a car as he skated across the brick streets.

Wadsworth residents did not regard his skating prowess as being worthy of monetary contributions, so Roy had to work to make a living. He did manual labor on a contractual basis and earned enough to maintain the life he lived. Seemingly, creature comforts were not important to him. It was rumored by those who lived near the square that he would wash up in the restroom of the east park gazebo on a somewhat regular basis.

For a time, he had a "shop" at 106 Bender's Court. We know the address because he painted it on a piece of wood and affixed it to the door frame. There he kept some tools, materials for repair work and anything else he needed to store. There seemed to be no limit to his skills. Whether he lived in the shop is in question.

He wore brown Carhart trousers and shirts, but when they were in the wash, he would wear nearly anything that would fit. He invariably wore boots, hip boots, stevedores or other types of work shoes appropriate for dirty jobs. He was physically powerful and in very good athletic shape, despite his obvious girth. Those who retained his services to dig ditches, spade gardens, clean out garages or basements or perform any other manual jobs were most complimentary about his work ethic, speed and honest effort.

One store owner hired him to dig a twenty-foot-long, two-foot-deep ditch at his residence from the sidewalk to his house. Roy accepted the job and started just before noon. At five o'clock, he walked into the store and announced to the owner that the ditch was dug. When the store owner asked him how much he wanted for the job, Roy said he wanted four dollars and fifty cents. The store owner gave him a five-dollar bill, but Roy refused it, explaining that he worked by the hour, he had worked four and a half hours and the quoted price was what he wanted. The store owner insisted, saying he should take the money since he had spent a half hour walking the lengthy trek from the owner's house to the store. Roy, who was as astute as he was strong, said he didn't subscribe to the portal-to-portal pay the coal miners were demanding, a reference to a long-lived issue debated in the mid-'40s between mine operators and miners who had disparate opinions about when their pay period should start.

Once, a popular Wadsworth teacher and coach engaged Roy in a discussion, thinking him to be somewhat unlettered and therefore easily overwhelmed by the teacher's erudition. What the teacher did not know—but soon learned—was that Roy read every newspaper he found in various places throughout town and read books he salvaged when he cleaned out garages and basements. A crowd gathered around, attracted by Roy's voice, which increased in pitch and volume as he felt the jab of playful arrogance coming from the teacher. It was not long before the teacher had to retreat in embarrassment, since Roy had documented facts that the teacher could not refute. Moving quickly from the platform of intellectual discourse to his usual demeanor, he uttered in a loud stage whisper: *"If you pull the tail of a jackass, figure on getting kicked."*

Roy had many poignant sayings that brought the topic of discussion to a quick focus. He seemed to favor comparisons with jackasses. In one discussion, he was heard to say to his adversary that *"a jackass born in Tennessee could go to Russia and be understood by a jackass born in Russia, and you're not understanding me and we're talking the same language."*

He was listening patiently as one of his clients asked him to do something that was difficult but insisted could be done. After listening for a few seconds, Roy blurted out, *"It would be easier for a drunk to swab the tonsils of a jackass with a toilet brush than to do what you're asking me to do."*

He had many cogent sayings that made one think. When discussing adversity, he once told his listener, "When you're in trouble, you have to lean on someone. You can't climb a ladder that's leaning toward you."

Once, when he became irritated because the person for whom he had worked did not pay him in a reasonable time, Ray told him he wanted his money by that Friday. The person asked what was so ironclad about Friday. Without hesitation, Roy rebutted, "Water don't flow uphill, and payday's on Friday. That's just the way Nature made it."

Roy was also a tap-dancer. While he did not tap on stage anymore so far as anyone was aware, it was not unusual for him to walk into a store and do a quick tap dance for clients to enjoy—in his stevedores! Clerks in the stores were accustomed to this, but shoppers sometimes weren't. It was not uncommon for Roy to do an encore, with or without applause. One clerk in a store that Roy frequented was always amazed because Roy would tap dance in the late afternoon, *after* a day of digging a ditch or dong some other hard labor. He seemed indefatigable.

There was a charming karma that existed between the community and Roy. The community would never have wanted to be without him. His somewhat individualized drumbeat was just that: different but charming.

It is thought by old-timers that one day Roy simply skated away, taking with him the cherished memories of his contribution to the Wadsworth fabric.

Philemon Kirkum

The Beauty in the Be[a]st

Just when we think we invented town characters and made legends out of them, we find the early history of Wadsworth highlighting one who earned that reputation in the days when the pioneers first settled here.

Philemon Kirkum was regarded as an eccentric native of Guilford, Connecticut. He fought in the Revolutionary War and, upon being severed from the military, decided to study law. In those days, lawyers did not need the extensive and exhaustive education that they do today. A student just had to read the law books and take a test to determine competency. Even the test was not too demanding.

Words taken from Boyd's *Annals of Winchester* credit Philemon with having several natural attributes that gave him an advantage in the courtroom: "He was tall in stature, erect of form, imposing in manner, fluent of speech, imaginative and impetuous." Additionally, he "was well-read, ingenuous in argument and oratorical in manner."

Unfortunately, he had some real lodestones to weigh him down. He had a quick temper, became enraged when questioned, was a poor loser, was without self-control and was the bane of judges' patience because of his errant behavior. After losing control time after time, he decided he should leave the practice of law, a decision cherished by judges and other members of the legal community. It is safe to assume that, with his reputation for irascibility, there were people in Guilford, Connecticut, who thought he should just leave.

The reasons for his unpopularity were not based entirely on behavior. He was an ultraliberal, out-of-control, almost socialistic Jeffersonian (Democrat)—this in a town that was straight-laced, conservative, uncompromising and straight-haired Federalist (Republican).

Philemon rode his horse around town dressed in his best finery and carried the banner for the farmers in the outlying areas as their party organizer and leader. So great was his zeal to espouse political liberalism that he opened a "Jeffersonian" store to oppose the Hinsdale Store (owned by ancestors of Wadsworth Hinsdale), which Philemon thought was bedecked with staid and unbending Federalist ideologies.

Of course, Philemon did not have the money to open the store—no one paid him for his political views—so he assembled about twenty or so people to give him capital. The investors allegedly named him manager of the store, but with Philemon's penchant for outbursts, his imposing physical frame and his eloquence, it was believed that he would have been the manager with or without approbation.

Philemon was not known for his humility. He erected a large billboard-type sign on his store that read, "Philemon Kirkum & Co." The sign itself was cause for much public disgrace in that there had never been a sign erected in Guilford, Connecticut, such as his.

The store did not flourish for long, given the fact that crowds of people gathered to buy the goods on a "free and easy business model"—equal distribution of wealth! After the store failed by losing money to people who were on the taking end of the distribution of wealth, Philemon thought better of trying any other type of venture in Guilford, Connecticut, so he started westward after trying his hand at law again and not succeeding. His old habits of ranting outbursts, loss of temper and arrogance did him in once again.

After weeks of travel with his wife and son, Philemon arrived at the Wadsworth settlement in a covered wagon pulled by a pair of oxen. He would not live here, however. Instead, for reasons known only to Philemon, he settled just across the north–south road, east of the "center," and took up residence in what would now be the Norton side of the north–south road. He did, however, frequent Wadsworth and was considered a resident of the newly formed settlement because of his constant presence here. There are some accounts of his having been on council in Norton, but, according to other accounts, he was only buried there. Twenty-one years after his death, he was buried with his wife, Polly, at Woodlawn Cemetery.

Philemon began farming but felt unfulfilled, so he went in search of some type of work that would utilize his verbal and intellectual skills. Not surprisingly, he was able to convince people that he should be a teacher, particularly since few people were lettered as much as he. Some accounts say he was an excellent teacher and dealt with children in a civil manner, probably because they knew better than to argue with him. Or perhaps it was because he made some adjustments in his life. He became less radical, less strident, less intense, more mild-mannered, more understanding and more pliable (on issues that didn't matter). Yet he continued with his eccentricities, still riding a horse in fine attire and demonstrating his handsome and manly physique to the admiring pioneers. It appeared that vanity was one quality he would not change.

Of the many things he left behind in Guilford, Connecticut, speaking ability was not one of them. He became known in Wadsworth as one of the best orators of the time—indeed, the best stump speaker—without the usual Jeffersonian rhetoric he had flailed at the people in Guilford. Pragmatic, Philemon began "stumping" on the ills of slavery, the rising of the South and the crumbling of the North—all issues that sat well with the straight-laced and usually Federalist-thinking people who settled here. He dropped his reputation as a persuasive jurist and featured himself as being a down-home farmer. This added to his credibility, but underneath, he reveled in going into town and letting the people know that this down-home boy was, infact, a brilliant, articulate, passionate and stalwart member of a conservative community. He was able to pull this off for the remainder of his ninety-one years, never weakening, even in old age.

People in Wadsworth held him up as a pillar of knowledge and erudition, never suspecting (or at least not caring if they did suspect) that he came here because he had irritated and agitated an entire community in Connecticut. A marker on his stone at Woodlawn Cemetery identifies him as a Revolutionary War veteran. Apparently, Wadsworth wanted to claim him as one of its own.

His legend continued for years, even into the twentieth century. In 1939, Wadsworth's 125th anniversary, Philemon Kirkum's name was read as one of Wadsworth's great legends. Philemon died in 1855; his wife, in 1839.

THE KREMER LEGACY

Marguerite Straiton, Culture in Eight Languages

Older residents of Wadsworth remember the Ephriam Kremer and Jonas Wuchter embalming stories. Jonas and Ephriam were both Pennsylvania Dutch, sharing the same traditions, attitudes and values; however, despite the same measure of strong conservative upbringing in their respective families, Ephriam veered a bit from the tradition and elected to bury Democrats, something Jonas reputedly did not or would not do. As a result of this division, Wadsworth had two embalmers in a community too small to otherwise warrant more than one. Since the majority of the population by this time was Federalist (Republican), Jonas worked more burials than Ephriam.

Ephriam's fame was not restricted to being the embalmer who buried Democrats; he was also one of the six founders of the German Reformed Church (now Trinity United Church of Christ). Ephriam married Lydia Everhard, of another early Wadsworth family, and they had only one son, Ellis. Ellis A. Kremer was born on April 1, 1862, and was a graduate of the University of Michigan Dental Department, a significant achievement at that time. (Most physicians, dentists and attorneys served apprenticeships with other physicians, dentists and attorneys and practiced after passing an exam.)

Ellis Kremer, a proud citizen and progenitor of a long line of outstanding community leaders in early Wadsworth, ending with Marguerite Straiton, his granddaughter.

Dr. Ellis married Minnie Sauder of Smithville, and they had four children. Their only daughter, Beulah Marguerite (forever known only as Marguerite), redefined the meaning of "legacy," despite the fact that she came from a long list of ancestors who were legacies in their own rights. Marguerite was a college graduate in the liberal arts, an extraordinary achievement for women in her day. With this distinction, she continued her father's prowess as a trailblazer. As indicated above, her father, Ellis, catapulted his father's nontraditional ways by becoming a university-educated dentist, the youngest (at age thirty-two) mayor ever to be elected to that position in Wadsworth's almost two-hundred-year history and the first person from Wadsworth to become chairman of the Medina County Democratic Party, a position he held for fifteen years. Marguerite was not to be outdone by these achievements; she created her own.

Marguerite was fortunate to have had a ready-made educational institution right in her own home. She listened intently as grandpa Ephriam and father Ellis talked about the events of the world, education, politics, professions and how life was to be lived. She remembered all of it and etched it indelibly into her mind, thinking that one day she would use it for what the Kremers stood for: giving to others what God has given to them.

Born in 1894, Marguerite never lived more than a block from the center of the village. Her home at 115 Maple Street was next door to the property where grandfather Ephriam built coffins and embalmed Democrats. Even though she had three brothers, her brothers are not mentioned in any of the literature about her, giving rise to the notion that she shone with such dignity that they paled in her presence.

According to her own words, Marguerite decided at age seven that she would devote her lifetime to study. When she died in 1989, she was still pursuing that goal. She was educated in the Wadsworth Schools and graduated from Wadsworth High School in 1912, one of twelve girls to do so in a class of seventeen. Typically, girls did not outnumber boys in the early part of the twentieth century, and when they did, they usually came from families that regarded education very highly. This was the case with Marguerite. Her family placed education higher than almost anything else. She went to Kent State University, and instead of doing what almost every other girl did at the time, she studied French and English rather than taking courses at the Kent Normal School to become a teacher.

Marguerite Kremer Straiton, a prolific poet, linguist and intellectual, gave of herself to those who did not have the luxury of what she considered a proper education.

Unsatisfied with knowing only two languages (English and French), Marguerite embarked on a lifetime study of other languages. When she had completed her self-imposed course of study, she was fluent in Spanish, German, Greek, Russian, Italian and Latin. She credits her love for language with the recognition that she was indefatigably articulate and that she needed several languages to enunciate the nuances of ideas stored in her head. With the ability to communicate in eight languages, she seemed satisfied that she could do so effectively.

One of the ways she used her gift of languages was in writing poetry. She was always interested in expressing her thoughts through this medium, but her passion grew even more after her husband, David Straiton, died. Before her own death in 1989, she had published 148 poems.

Marguerite did not write silly or frivolous poems; they were all serious and thoughtful works. She wrote about life, duty, love, morality and nature. After Dave died, she wrote poems about what life meant to her, what death would mean to her and the unknown life hereafter.

Writing poetry was not her only bent; she also wrote an unusual account of the life of Jesus Christ. She spent many years doing research and detailed her findings in a book that had Jesus speaking in the first person, giving details that made Him human and offering thoughts about how He felt about being God. When she read the book to her art and history class, she observed that the ladies paused their knitting to listen to her presentation.

Dave and Marguerite had no children, but Marguerite endeavored to educate all of the neighborhood children, citing as her motivation for doing so the fact that most of their parents were not taking education seriously. She believed people were not interested in developing minds, duty, responsibility, correct attitudes or behaviors. She felt the generation of her day had abdicated its role in fostering and nurturing all of these traits, and without them, the children would be ill-equipped to function as contributing citizens in later life. With her gift of knowledge, her ability to communicate effectively and her desire to impart knowledge to the masses, she felt she had a duty to educate anyone who was within her reach.

In the 1930s, Marguerite spent countless evenings at Franklin School teaching immigrants what they needed to know to become citizens. With her command of eight languages, she was able to communicate with nearly everyone in his or her own language and, at the same time, teach the aspiring citizens to speak English. Almost all of her foreign students are deceased now, but when they were alive, they maintained an undying indebtedness to her compassion and patience—and owed passing the citizenship exam to her.

Marguerite had a strong sense of what was right or wrong, what was in good taste and what was not, what was proper decorum and what was inappropriate, what was morally acceptable and what was against the tenets of morality and what was truth and what was not. She felt people should speak out against anything they thought to be against the grain of propriety. She was certain she was doing so. She was aware that others thought she

Marguerite Straiton (far right) taught scores of immigrants who were preparing to become American citizens.

was difficult and opinionated, but she thought what she was doing was the right thing to do. She believed her opinions opened people's eyes to truth, righteousness, beauty and the natural order of things.

Marguerite was always dressed properly, with gloves, perfect grooming and evidence of impeccably good manners. She ate two meals a day at a local restaurant, with Dave accompanying her for the evening meal. She was aware that people thought she was putting on airs by her demeanor, dress and the fact that she ate out instead of eating at home. Her rebuttal was simple: her kitchen was always immaculate, and she did not need to defend appropriate dress or manners.

There was never any food in the house except for sweets she would give to the children who came to her porch to listen to her read her poems. She thought the children did not come for the candy but to enrich their minds, since their parents did not do this for them. She felt it was her Christian duty to give of her talents to the children since they would be the future of the world, and without knowledge of what was beautiful, they would be deficient in life skills.

Marguerite died in 1989, but before she died, she suffered a severe blow to what she thought should be her legacy. She had hoped to enshrine her home as the ancestral home of the Kremer family, a family that rowed against the tide. The City of Wadsworth purchased her home, razed it and made the property into a parking lot.

Marguerite's home—the home of her ancestors—no longer stands. But what does stand is the legacy of her poetry, her book on Jesus speaking in the first person and the memory of a woman who knew what was right and proper and could speak her mind in eight languages.

BIBLIOGRAPHY

Boyd, John. *Annals of Winchester*. Winchester, CT: City of Winchester, 1873.

Brown, Edward. *Wadsworth Memorial*. Wadsworth, OH: Steam Printing House, 1875.

Dietrich, Phil. "A Pioneer Hit the Dirt." *Akron Beacon Journal*, July 18, 1965.

General Ordinances of the City of Wadsworth. Wadsworth, OH: Steam Printing House, 1876.

Hinsdale, Mary L., ed. *Garfield-Hinsdale Letters*. Ann Arbor: University of Michigan Press, 1949.

Historical Atlas of Medina County Ohio. Chicago: L.H. Everts & Co., 1874.

Map of Wadsworth. Cleveland, OH: Frank Krause, ca. 1850.

Map of Wadsworth Township. N.p., ca. 1875.

Match Tips. A House Organ of the Ohio Match Company. May 1934.

McGraw, Arthur W. *First Official State Map*. Vol. V. Columbus: Ohio Archaeological and Historical Publications, 1804.

Rohrer, Anna Lois. *Mennonites of Medina County*. Wadsworth, OH: Bethel Mennonite Church, 1982.

Schapiro, Eleanor Iler. *Wadsworth Heritage*. Wadsworth, OH: Wadsworth News-Banner, 1964.

Siebert, William H. *The Mysteries of Ohio's Underground Railroads: Ohio's Underground Trails*. Columbus, OH: Arthur W. McGraw, 1993. Reprint.

Taylor, David A. *Soul of a People: The WPA Writers Project uncovers Depression America*. Hoboken, NJ: Wiley, 2009.

Wadsworth Banner-Press, January 23, 1919; September 21, 1922; November 7, 1929; August 27, 1931.

Wadsworth Village Cemetery. *Rules and Regulations*. Wadsworth, OH: Steam Printing House, 1878.

Wadsworth Village Plat Map. N.p., ca. 1875.

Westenbarger, Zachary Taylor. Unpublished journal, n.d.

Writers' Program. *Ohio Guide*. New York: Oxford University Press, 1940.

INTERVIEWS

James Haynes, March 19, 2010

Virginia Haynes, April 7, 2010

Peter Hoffman, 2007

Raymond Holcomb, February 17, 2010

Daniel Weltzein, March 29, 2010

Glen Westenbarger, March 17, 2010

ABOUT THE AUTHOR

Caesar and Lynda Carrino.

Born in Wadsworth, Ohio, on January 5, 1931, Caesar Carrino attended Wadsworth schools, graduating in 1948. He entered Baldwin-Wallace College and received an education degree in 1952 before serving in the Korean War. He earned a master's degree from the University of Akron and a PhD from Case-Western Reserve University following military service.

Beginning in 1954, he taught in the Norton Schools, where he became principal in 1956; functioned as a supervisor in Summit County Schools in 1966; and joined the University of Akron in 1967. In 1970, he became assistant to the dean of the College of Education and assistant dean in 1972. He was promoted to dean of the Evening College and Summer Sessions in 1974. He retired in 1989.

Following retirement, he trained industrialists, served as principal in two schools, became a high school chancellor, advised at-risk students, directed a professional education unit and became mayor of Wadsworth in 2000.

Presently, he works with Historic Downtown Wadsworth to help preserve its historic integrity and reviews university programs for accreditation.